T0207730

More Mary's Musings

Endless Blessings

MARY KULA ZOELLER

WESTBOW
PRESS®
A DIVISION OF THOMAS NELSON
& ZONDERVAN

WestBow Press books may be ordered through booksellers or by contacting:

WestBow Press
A Division of Thomas Nelson & Zondervan
1663 Liberty Drive
Bloomington, IN 47403
www.westbowpress.com
1 (866) 928-1240

ISBN: 978-1-9736-7428-3 (sc)
ISBN: 978-1-9736-7430-6 (hc)
ISBN: 978-1-9736-7429-0 (e)

Library of Congress Control Number: 2019914404

Print information available on the last page.

WestBow Press rev. date: 9/24/2019

Dedication

I have to give at least partial credit for this book to my friend, Alison's, 95 year old mother. She only had three more pages to read of Mary's Musings and wanted to read more. When she asked her daughter to tell me to please write fast, it touched my heart.

Appreciation

Sometimes life gets busy and we forget to say how much the people in our lives mean to us. So, to my husband, Michael, for his love, help, and support, and to my children and grandchildren, please remember how very much I love you. You all have a special place in my heart.

Introduction

A number of people have asked me if I was going to write another book. My response has always been probably not.

I wasn't sure it would happen, but once I started writing, stories poured out of me. I never dreamed I'd write a second book, but then I never knew I'd write the first one.

I have shared more musings that continue to remind me of the numerous blessings God has given me. As in my first book, I've included scriptures, a brief memory, a few short words of prayer, and some song thoughts.

Once again, I hope you can take a couple minutes each day to find some daily inspiration.

1—Learning to Know God

> He who finds a wife finds a good thing, And obtains
> favor from the Lord. (Proverbs 18:22 NKJV)

After one final walk-through of our daughter's wedding ceremony, we could head to the rehearsal dinner. Then I heard my husband say, "What if I don't want to give her away? Can't we just keep her?"

I always cry at weddings. That afternoon I was determined to hold myself together. Our once baby girl was now a beautiful bride.

Prior to exchanging rings, the couple took a moment to read the vows they had written to each other. Stating the many reasons he had fallen in love with my daughter, the groom ended his words by saying, "She helped me to know God."

Tears slipped down my cheeks as a small voice inside me said, "You must have done something right while raising your little girl. Thank you, Lord."

Father, we strive to raise our children to follow you, yet sometimes in retrospect we feel we should have done so much more. Please help us to always do our best, as we look to you for guidance.

Song Thoughts

" 'Tis so sweet to trust in Jesus, just to take him at his word."

2—Life's Miracles

You will keep in perfect peace all who trust in you, all whose thoughts are fixed on you. Trust in the Lord always, for the Lord God is eternal rock. (Isaiah 26:3–4 NLT)

I was on my way to the hospital to pick up my mother and take her home. As I drove through the intersection, I noticed a car coming toward me. The driver, having fallen asleep, ran through the red light and smashed into the side of my car. That pushed me into another car.

My mother, who had been watching for me, saw the whole thing from her hospital window. It was a scary scene. Thankfully, Mom was able to calm down, and the doctor released her into my care. The tow truck driver gave us a ride home, and then he dropped my car off at the local body shop.

The next day I went to the body shop to see what damage had been done to my car. I had been told the vehicle was totaled. While I was looking at the crushed mess, a man walked up to me and commented, "No one got out of that car alive."

I replied, "Yes, I did."

Thank you, Father, for always watching over us every minute and for sending angels to guard us each day as we follow you.

Song Thoughts

"God is good all the time. He puts a song
of praise in this heart of mine."

3—Guardian Angels

> Now all these things happened unto them for examples: and they are written for our admonition, upon whom the ends of the world are come. (1 Corinthians 10:11 KJV)

Since I started school I've been an avid reader. I've always loved books. My family watched a little TV, but more often than not, if I had the opportunity, my nose was stuck in a book. I had four siblings, and we were usually outside on sunny days or downstairs playing when it rained.

I rarely had any quiet time by myself to read. Since my parents always sent us to bed early, or so it seemed to one so young, I would dim the bedside lamp with my chenille robe and proceed to read. Many times I'd get so caught up in what I was reading I'd become oblivious to anything happening around me.

Thankfully, that evening, my parents smelled something burning and started searching the house. Seeing some light, they rushed into our bedroom. There they found a big, dark-brown, scorched spot on my robe about to burst into flames.

Heavenly Father, please help us to heed instruction. Help us to learn from our mistakes and make better decisions and choices each time.

Song Thoughts

"The wise man built his house upon the rock
and the house on the rock stood firm."

4—Rejoicing in Heaven

> Whoever believes and is baptized will be saved, but whoever does not believe will be condemned. (Mark 16:16 NIV)

"James is being baptized at church camp on Friday, but Elise says she might wait until Sunday," my daughter excitedly announced.

"Hallelujah! We'll be there." I happily responded.

Right after I hung up the phone, my other daughter called. "Guess who is being baptized at church camp?" Her son had also accepted Jesus as his Lord and Savior.

Absolutely thrilled, I answered the phone again to hear my son inform me that his daughter, Grace, was also being baptized. Praise the Lord!

Our hearts were overflowing with happiness as four grandchildren became immersed believers. My friend smiled as she said, "That day is one of the perks of grandparenthood."

Father, we know Jesus died for our sins, and there is great rejoicing in the presence of angels when even one sinner repents. Thank you for loving us and sending Jesus.

Song Thoughts

"Have you been to Jesus for the cleansing power?
Are you washed in the blood of the lamb?"

5—For of Such is the Kingdom of Heaven

And he took the children in his arms, placed his hands
on them and blessed them. (Mark 10:16 NIV)

"**C**an I go outside and get the stink blown off?" one of the boys in my
day care asked. I had to laugh. I love little kids.

When I was younger, my neighbor called me Mother Mary. She
loved it when I'd come to her house. I'd change diapers, feed, and
sometimes bathe her baby.

One day, while I was working in the church office, the pastor asked
me, "If you could choose any job and didn't have to think about how
much money you were making, what would you want to do?"

Without hesitating, I replied, "Sit and rock babies!"

Mothers were constantly calling our church office to inquire
if we had anyone in our congregation who provided child care. I've
always loved babies and little kids, so one thing led to another. I ended
up running a daycare out of my home for ten years, though I never
advertised. Simply by word of mouth, my business grew. I always had
plenty of children in my care.

Dear Lord, we are so blessed. We are especially happy when we love
our jobs. Thank you for the talents you give us and happiness that is
ours when we help others.

Song Thoughts

"Jesus loves the little children, all the children of the world.
They are precious in His sight."

6—Be Wise

> Though the fig tree does not bud and there are no grapes on the vines, though the olive crop fails and the fields produce no food, though there are no sheep in the pen and no cattle in the stalls, yet I will rejoice in the Lord, I will be joyful in God my Savior. (Habakkuk 3:17–18 NIV)

Our son wanted to be a garbage man so that he could jump off and onto the truck while going from house to house each day. My daughter repeatedly told us that when she got old enough, she wanted to work at the Gold Circle department store. The cash register fascinated her. We never really knew why.

One day we heard a young man make a similar remark. His reasoning was that he thought you could take the cash register drawer home with you at the end of the day. How cool would that be? Ha, ha. He didn't realize the cashiers were taking the money to the store office. He just saw employees pick up the drawers of money and walk away.

That is not the way it works, unfortunately. You have to wait for your paycheck. My daughter says that was not her reason, but it might have been a good enticement.

Heavenly Father, we know things are not always as they seem. Please help us to be happy and to find joy in each day of life you give us.

Song Thoughts

"I'm happy to be in the truth, for I will always
sing of when your love came down."

7—Uniquely Different

> For you created my inmost being; you knit me together
> in my mother's womb. I praise you because I am fearfully
> and wonderfully made; your works are wonderful, I
> know that full well. (Psalm 139:13–14 NIV)

My two little blond children and I sat down on a bench in the mall. We were taking a short rest, and I had given the kids a treat for being so well-behaved. I picked up their dark haired baby sister from the stroller to snuggle and hug her, too.

A fellow shopper stopped to exclaim, "What a beautiful baby. Is she adopted?"

When my reply was no, and I explained that my husband had dark hair, she proceeded to insinuate that I was lying.

"There's no way someone with your coloring and two other blond-haired children could have a baby with hair that dark," she said, prancing away.

"Well, I gave birth to her!" I hollered.

We thank you Father, for the blessing of each new child. Thank you for creating each of us uniquely and for a special purpose.

Song Thoughts

"You are the potter, I am the clay. Mold me
and make me, this is what I pray."

8—Secure in His Love

> Do not boast about tomorrow, for you do not know what a day may bring forth. (Proverbs 27:1 NKJV)

We didn't turn on the radio or television first thing that September 11 morning after awakening. Actually, we tried to be quiet since our youngest daughter was not feeling well. Thinking that she probably had a flu bug, I left her sleeping and kept her home from school.

My husband headed off to work, and I went to my room to choose my outfit for the day. I wouldn't be going anywhere. I'd spend the day with my sick little girl.

Shortly thereafter, the telephone rang. My husband called to tell me about an airplane crashing into the twin towers of the World Trade Center in New York City. He said that I might want to turn on the television. Another hijacked plane had crashed into the Pentagon in Washington DC.

What? Are you serious? How could this be? Was this the end of the world? I was so thankful that my child was home with me and as safe as possible. The rest of that day is a blur.

Thank you, Father, for your promise to always be with us. Please strengthen and renew our trust in you as we seek your guidance and protection in our lives each day.

Song Thoughts

"Let the King of my heart be the mountain where I run,
be the shadow where I hide."

9—Enjoying Every Moment

Not that I was ever in need, for I have learned how
to get along happily whether I have much or little.
(Philippians 4:11 TLB)

E ven though we had to take her out of school, it seemed like a wonderful
idea to take our young daughter to Disney World in Florida. January
was the perfect, non-busy time of year to go.

While we were at Universal Studios, my daughter was chosen to be
on television. Several of her school classmates saw her on TV. She was
the Slime Time victim, I mean contestant, on Nickelodeon.

First, our daughter earned a pie in the face. Then, she and her team
partner won the contest which meant they had a ton of green slime
dumped over their heads. Eww... Lastly, they were blasted with the Big
Shaboozie.

The girls won and were given signed t-shirts. As we left the studio
my daughter exclaimed, "That was the best day of my life."

Heavenly Father, thank you so much for the many blessings you
pour out day after day. You give us so much more than we deserve.

Song Thoughts

"Your praise will ever be on my lips, ever be on my lips."

10—He Restores My Soul

> Keep your lives free from the love of money and be
> content with what you have, because God has said,
> "Never will I leave you; never will I forsake you."
> (Hebrews 13:15 NIV)

I loved to hear the wind blowing through the trees in the woods behind
our house. Initially, it kept me awake. One night I started thinking of
it as God being near me. He wasn't marching in the mulberry trees like
in says in the book of Samuel, but he was definitely close by. I drifted
into sleep in a state of tranquil serenity.

A few years later when we moved, I could no longer hear the wind
fanning through the trees. I missed the feeling that God was by my side.
I was unable to fall asleep peacefully.

Trying to think of other relaxing sounds brought the ocean to mind.
I love hearing the waves washing onto the shoreline.

We bought a small waterfall to set on the dresser. The sound of
water repeatedly trickling over a few small rocks is very peaceful.

I can't help but recall the scripture in Matthew 8:27 NIV. The men
were amazed and asked, "What kind of man is this? Even the winds and
the waves obey him!"

What a blessing it is, Father, just knowing that you have promised
to be with us every day and throughout the night. Thank you for the
love and peace you give us.

Song Thoughts

"Let me be singing when the evening comes,
bless the Lord oh my soul."

11—Learning to Drive

I will instruct you and teach you in the way you should go; I will counsel you with my loving eye on you. (Psalm 32:8 NIV)

I could hardly wait to learn to drive. My Driver's Education Teacher was Mr. Jordan. He also coached the high school basketball team. He gave me the nickname Highway Hilda and jokingly called my friend Hotrod Harriet. Even so, we both finished the course with an A+.

On hot days Coach would tell us to drive to the local <u>East Canton Dairyette</u>. There he would treat us to soft serve chocolate ice cream cones. I don't remember why, but we laughingly began calling them brown whirly-whips.

After I obtained my driver's license, my parents helped me buy a used car with a stick shift and a clutch. It was not my first choice of vehicles, but now I had my own car.

One afternoon my sister and I decided to go visit our friends. I was doing fine until we came to a red light at the top of a small hill. When the light turned green I tried to go, but my car kept stalling.

After several repeated attempts, the man in the pick-up truck behind me came up to my car and rapped on the window. Being cautious of strangers I only lowered my window an inch, enough to hear him say, "It might help if you put it into first gear instead of third."

He walked back to his truck, and the light turned green. Totally embarrassed, I put my car into first gear, punched the gas and took off.

So many times we fail and fall short. Thank you, Father, for your mercy and grace, and for those you send to help us along the way.

Song Thoughts

"Amazing grace, how sweet the sound, was blind but now I see."

12–*Fear of Failure*

> Don't worry about anything; instead, pray about
> everything. Tell God what you need, and thank him
> for all he has done. Then you will experience God's
> peace, which exceeds anything we can understand.
> His peace will guard your hearts and minds as you live
> in Christ Jesus. (Philippians 4:6–7 NLT)

Growing up, my goal was to please my parents and make them happy. When they said jump, I asked, "How high?"

If I accidentally did the wrong thing, I was corrected. My tears began to fall. It occurred so often, that my mom told me if I didn't stop crying so much, she was going to have to take me to the hospital to have surgery on my tear bags.

For dinner every day we had meat, potatoes, and some kind of vegetable. One rare evening, instead of a regular potato dish, we had potato chips! I couldn't stop eating them.

Since I sat on my dad's right, he saw that the meat and veggies on my plate were practically untouched. He told me to not eat another potato chip until I ate some of my other food.

"Okay." I replied, as the tears began rolling down my cheeks. I picked up another potato chip and stuck it in my mouth before realizing what I had done.

Dad looked at my mom and grinned. I quickly scooped up a spoonful of peas and shoved them into my mouth.

Heavenly Father, we long to live perfect lives for you, yet so many times we fall into sin. Please forgive us and draw us closer to you.

Song Thoughts

"Here is my heart Lord, I lay it open, slow
in your anger, rich in your love."

13—Loving Mother Nature

For they refreshed my spirit and yours also. Such men deserve recognition. (1 Corinthians 16:18 NIV)

We lived in the country. There were a lot of trees and even a small creek. Dad would wander through the woods with us until he found a strong enough vine wrapped around a tree that we could use as our Tarzan rope. It worked best when there was plenty of space for us to swing. The vine usually remained strong for year or so, but when it broke dad would find another one for us.

There were tons of pine cones and lots of wild flowers like Johnny Jump-ups. The forest was our version of a glorified playground. Dad built a rustic bridge across the creek, although it wasn't necessary, since we could mostly just step on some rocks to cross.

On really hot days, when dad wasn't available to be our lifeguard so we could go swimming in the lake, we would dam up a small area of the creek to make it deeper. Then we'd take turns, one person at a time, sitting in the water to cool off.

We thank you, heavenly Father, for our families as well as all the little things you've created for our enjoyment.

Song Thoughts

"Precious memories, how they linger, how they ever flood my soul."

14—Kids Will Be Kids

> For I know the plans I have for you," declares the Lord, "plans to prosper you and not to harm you, plans to give you hope and a future. (Jeremiah 29:11 NIV)

When it was just my older sister and me, plus one baby sister, we lived only minutes from my grandma and grandpa. While mom was busy with things around the house or feeding the baby, we would sometimes wander down the tar road to go visit our grandma.

One day, we even wore our little rubber boots. When they got stuck in the tar, we simply stepped out of them and continued on our way in our bare feet. When we got to grandma's house, she washed our feet with turpentine to remove the tar! Ewww...

Once when I was even younger, my sister rocked me in an old rocking chair that was in one of grandma's upstairs bedrooms. We accidentally went backwards through the window, chair and all. Thankfully for us, the back of the rockers caught on the window sill. My sister hung on to me tightly while she yelled, and we waited for someone to rescue us. I giggled. It must have been fun.

Thank you, Father, for always watching over us and keeping us safe. Most of all, thank you for loving us.

Song Thoughts

"Praise Him! Praise Him! Jesus, our blessed Redeemer."

15—The Wrong Way

> Be still before the Lord and wait patiently for him; do
> not fret when people succeed in their ways, when they
> carry out their wicked schemes. (Psalm 37:7 NIV)

A rriving in London late one evening, we were looking for a bus to
take us to the St. Giles Hotel on Oxford Street. We tried questioning
the driver of the bus at the curb, but his response was to grab our bags,
throw them into the storage area, and growl at us to get on the bus. We
quickly obeyed.

After driving for more than an hour, I questioned the girl sitting in
front of me concerning our destination. A college student, she told me
that we were on our way to St. Giles Street in Oxford, England. They
were all heading back to school at the University of Oxford.

Since she knew the driver somewhat, from previous trips to and
from the campus, she walked up to the front to tell him about our
dilemma. He rudely told her that he knew we were on the wrong bus!

At 1:00 a.m. the bus driver dropped everyone else off at Oxford
University. We were taken to the station to wait for the next bus that
would take us back to our hotel. At least they didn't make us buy another
ticket.

It isn't always easy to overlook mistakes and forgive people, yet we
know, Lord, that you repeatedly forgive us of our sins and continue to
love us. Please help us to become more Christ-like.

Song Thoughts

"Everyone needs forgiveness, the kindness of a Savior.
He can move the mountains, my God is mighty to save."

16—Mistakes and Mercies

> But he said to me, "My grace is sufficient for you, for my power is made perfect in weakness." Therefore I will boast all the more gladly about my weaknesses, so that Christ's power may rest on me. (2 Corinthians 12:9 NIV)

My husband's mother lives in Germany. When my husband goes to Europe for work, I usually try to go along so we can visit her. Since airline tickets are not very cheap, we always plan to stay at least two weeks. Sometimes we add in a little side trip while we are there.

On one trip we were blessed with the opportunity to visit Austria. We walked around Salzburg while waiting for our Sound of Music tour.

Since we had time we decided to take a horse and buggy ride. When the driver headed down the street where we had parked our rental car, we were shocked to see the area totally empty. Not a single car could be seen.

We explained to our driver that our rental car was gone. He was not surprised and told us that no parking was allowed in that area after lunchtime. We had not read the small print on the parking ticket we had purchased.

At the end of our carriage ride, we were kindly dropped at the police station to pay the fine. Then, we hurriedly took a bus out of town to the place where our car had been towed. We barely made it back in time to board the Sound of Music bus for our tour.

Father, we make so many mistakes in our lives. Thank you for forgiving us and giving us the strength to go on for another day.

Song Thoughts

"Great is thy faithfulness. Morning by morning new mercies I see."

17–Decisions, Decisions

> He has shown you, O mortal, what is good. And what
> does the Lord require of you? To act justly and to love
> mercy and to walk humbly with your God. (Micah
> 6:8 NIV)

My husband is such a diligent worker. His boss asked what they could do to make him happy, making a point to tell him how much they valued his work, emphasizing that they did not want to lose him. What a wonderful compliment.

They gave him a promotion including a lump sum bonus. As much as I want to return to my home state of Ohio, it sure makes it difficult to even consider moving.

I've accepted the fact that this is where God wants us, at least for now. My daughter says, "Michael doesn't want to move us back to Ohio because he doesn't want to share me."

Michael says, "That's right."

Returning to Ohio is still on my agenda. Tee hee.

Please help us to use our talents diligently, Father, in ways that would be pleasing to you.

Song Thoughts

"There's a new name written down in glory
and it's mine, oh yes it's mine."

18—Filled With Laughter

A time to weep and a time to laugh; a time to mourn and a time to dance. (Ecclesiastes 3:4 NIV)

We were excitedly waiting in our seats for everything to begin. It was the year's end pre-school program.

As the little ones walked onto the stage some of them waved to the people they knew. The pianist began to play. The children's attention was drawn to their director, and they happily began singing, doing the motions as their leader directed.

With a big smile on my face, I proudly watched as my two grandsons grinned and started singing <u>Thank You, Lord</u>. When the song ended, everyone clapped. Allen started bowing so energetically that he almost turned a somersault off of the stage platform. Surprisingly, he had great balance and didn't fall.

Too bad we didn't have the right camera with us. His family surely would have won $10,000 for America's Funniest Home Videos. We laughed and laughed.

We love you, Lord, and we praise your name with joyful hearts. We are so blessed.

Song Thoughts

"Shout for joy, see what love has done. He has come for us, He's the saving one."

19—Making the Best of Things

> God has given each of you some special abilities; be
> sure to use them to help each other, passing on to
> others God's many kinds of blessings. (1Peter 4:10 TLB)

My daughter appeared to have adjusted well to our move to New
York. She jumped right in and ran for Student Council, played girls'
basketball, and was one of ten sixth graders chosen to go for a fiction
writing work-shop at the Rensselaer Institute of Technology.

She tried out for drama club and won a role in the <u>Annie</u> musical.
She always got straight A's on her report card.

One afternoon, she organized the closet in her bedroom according
to colors of her clothes. Even though I'm her mother, I was very impressed
with everything.

While I was talking to my friend on the telephone, my daughter
overheard me saying that I thought she liked it here in New York.

She quickly corrected me. "I never said that I liked it here. I just
get bored."

Father, you give us so many talents and abundant blessings day after
day. Help us to use them wisely and to follow in the footsteps you lay
before us.

Song Thoughts

"May the words I say and the things I do,
make my life song bring a smile to you."

20—Showing Your Love

> And whatever you do, whether in word or deed, do it
> all in the name of the Lord Jesus, giving thanks to God
> the Father through him. (Colossians 3:17 NIV)

Michele wanted to stay home and care for her newborn baby, but needed the extra income of a job. I know personally what a special time this can be for a mother. I wanted it to be a wonderful bonding experience for her and her son, too.

I decided to help by allowing her to manage my daycare while I took a position from October to March with a temp agency where my friend worked. In return, Michele agreed to watch my four year old daughter.

Missing me, my daughter asked, "Why does mommy leave so early in the morning when it's dark and then not come home again until it gets dark?"

Michele said, "To earn money."

My daughter seriously replied, "Why doesn't she just go on Wheel of Fortune?"

Father, we know things aren't always as easy or as simple as they might seem. Please help us to make the right choices and love others like Jesus loves us.

Song Thoughts

"How great, how great, how great is your love."

21—Saturday Fun Day

> Instead be filled with the Spirit, speaking to one another with psalms, hymns, and songs from the Spirit. Sing and make music from your heart to the Lord. (Ephesians 5:18–19 NIV)

Saturday mornings were one of my sisters' and my favorite times. We regularly went for Junior Choir practice at our church. We loved learning how to harmonize parts in a song. Our director would always find new music for us to sing. We never got bored.

Often after choir practices, a bunch of us kids would help prepare the Sunday bulletins by folding and stuffing them. It gave us more time to hang out with each other, laughing and talking.

One Saturday the pastor asked me how much I weighed. I wasn't very big, though I don't remember my weight at that time. He got down on the floor and asked me to walk on his back. He instructed me as to how I should move up and down his spine sideways, keeping my feet close together.

He had evidently sized me up pretty well, and it must have helped him get the kinks out, because I did it more Saturdays than just that one time.

We know our bodies are wonderfully made and we praise you, Lord. The way they work is simply amazing.

Song Thoughts

"It's your breath in our lungs, so we pour out our praise. You give life, you are love. Great are you Lord."

22–Onward Christian Soldiers

Make a joyful noise unto the Lord, all ye lands. Serve the Lord with gladness: come before His presence with singing. (Psalm 100:2 NIV)

I can remember singing songs from the time I could talk. I'm pretty sure I knew my ABC's from singing <u>The Alphabet Song</u> and how to count by singing <u>Ten Little Indians</u>.

Singing is the way I memorized the books of the Bible. It's also how I learned the names of all fifty states. I wish there was a song to learn all the state capitals.

My family pretty much sang constantly, especially while doing chores like washing dishes and traveling in the car. Occasionally dad would sing with us, but he was not very adept at matching the words with the notes.

Dad's favorite song was <u>Onward Christian Soldiers</u>. He memorized the words and he knew the tune, but as we girls sang, he would trail behind, struggling to get in sync. By the end of the first verse, he was unable to keep up with us and sang 'forward into baaattle, see his banner go... awww rats.' Everyone was laughing as we began to sing verse two.

We praise you heavenly Father and look forward to singing with the angels in glory.

Song Thoughts

"I heard a million voices praise the name of Jesus, singing in God's choir in the sky."

23–He Hears Our Prayers

A faithful man will abound with blessings, but he who
hastens to be rich will not go unpunished. (Proverbs
28:20 NKJV)

My husband's company was sending him to Beijing for work. It was
his first time to China. Fellow employees who had traveled there
before were concerned about the weather and how it might affect their
health. Beijing's normal daily forecast was for smog and air pollution.
My husband's boss returned from a previous work trip with a bad lung
infection.

My daily prayers prior to Michael and his co-workers leaving for
Beijing were that they would have a safe trip. I also prayed that none of
them would be affected health-wise.

Rejoicing upon their return, I was told that while they were there,
Beijing had the best air quality index they had seen in the past 35 years.
Wow! There were no doubts in my mind that God had answered my
prayers in an incredible way. Our God is awesome!

Thank you so much for the power of prayer. You hear our cries for
help and answer in amazing ways showing us your love. We praise you.

Song Thoughts

"The Lord has promised good to me, His word my hope secures.
He will my shield and portion be as long as life endures."

24—God is Always With Us

> Keep me safe, my God, for in you I take refuge. (Psalm 16:1 NIV)

During our first warm and sunny spring day together as husband and wife, Michael was excited to show off his Ducati. I am not a fan of motorcycles so I can't say I was looking forward to the ride. Since I knew it would make him happy, I agreed to the trip.

My dad, and several other people I knew, had been seriously injured while riding motorcycles. My cousin, as well as my good friend's brother, had been killed on motorcycles. None of those accidents were their fault.

Our ride didn't start out well since Michael couldn't find the smaller helmet for me to wear, but off we went. I felt like I was a bobble-head, and I was hanging on for dear life.

Every time we stopped, the big helmet I was wearing crashed my head into his helmet. As we zoomed up the road I couldn't help but worry what might happen if I knocked him out. If that happened, then I knew we were in serious trouble because I didn't know anything about motorcycles.

Thankfully, we had a safe trip. I must admit that it was kind of fun, but knowing my fears, my husband soon sold his motorcycle. Whew!

We're so thankful that you have promised to always be with us and watch over us. Please help us to make wise decisions.

Song Thoughts

"Never once did we ever walk alone, never once did you leave us on our own, God you are faithful."

25–Always Keep Smiling

A cheerful heart is good medicine, but a broken spirit
saps a person's strength. (Proverbs 17:22 NLT)

My neurologist appointments are always interesting, to say the least. On one visit I was asked, "Do you think you have any problem remembering things?"

I quickly responded, saying, "If I do, I don't remember." My husband and the doctor immediately began laughing.

At another visit, my neurologist shared how he took his friend's driving test for him about fifty years ago. If his friend passed the test his dad had agreed to buy him a VW minivan, so that he and his buddies could take a road trip across the United States.

During a more recent appointment my neurologist asked, "Why do you think you're doing so well?"

I replied, "I try to eat healthy, exercise every day, and I pray a lot."

My doctor gave me a big hug and said, "Mary, you're the best."

Thank you, Father, for life here on earth and for the people that cross our paths. Most of all, we praise you for giving us the opportunity of everlasting life with you.

Song Thoughts

"Your love never fails, and never gives up. It never runs out on me."

26—Give it Your Best Shot

> But you are a chosen people, a royal priesthood, a holy
> nation, God's special possession, that you may declare
> the praises of him who called you out of darkness into
> his wonderful light. (1 Peter 2:9 NIV)

I loved going to church camp. After attending several years as a young
camper, I volunteered to help as a staff member for as many weeks as
I could.

Each evening we had Vesper services up on a hillside. It was so
peaceful. We'd sing and listen to a sermon. I'll never forget the evening
I was asked to sing a verse from a hymn chosen to close the service. At
the end of the final chorus I forgot the words, 'till my raptured soul shall
find rest beyond the river,' so I substituted, 'Jesus keep me near the cross
in your love forever.' No one commented. Maybe they didn't notice.

A friend I met as a camper when I was fifteen years old thought
she would like to work at camp. I suggested she tell her pastor about her
willingness. She told me that he said she was too young; a person had to
be sixteen. Uh oh. I'd been working as a volunteer for two years!

Thank you, Father, for the opportunities you send our way. Help us
to know you better and learn to love you more.

Song Thoughts

"Now your mercy has saved my soul.
Now your freedom is all that I know.
The old made new."

27—Life Abundant

> Lazy hands make for poverty, but diligent hands bring
> wealth. (Proverbs 10:4 NIV)

My husband loves working outside in our yard. When he took the
trash out, it seemed to take forever. Finally he came back inside,
and shared that he had meandered around the yard just picking up
some twigs.

It had been a long cold winter. I even heard someone say it was
minus zero degrees, whatever that is. Ha, ha. Being that cold, we had
a couple dustings of snow, but my husband rarely got to use his snow
blower.

That night we were pounded with almost twelve inches of snow. I
noticed our neighbor man had hired a man who had a plow on the front
of his truck. I quickly suggested that my husband walk across the street,
and ask him to clear our driveway, too.

"Then what's the use of owning a snow blower?" my husband replied,
as he smiled. Boys and their toys. LOL.

Please help me, Lord, to truly appreciate all the blessings that I so
often fail to even notice. I know that I'm richly blessed.

Song Thoughts

"Blessed assurance, Jesus is mine, this is my story, this is my song."

28—Trusting Jesus

> I call on you, my God, for you will answer me; turn
> your ear to me and hear my prayer. (Psalm 17:6 NIV)

Our church started a building campaign. Everyone was asked to give donations, and to make a promise to give a certain amount of their income for the duration of our church expansion.

Being recently married and just starting out, money wasn't abundant. Even so, my husband and I felt the desire in our heart to make a pledge. Having no idea where we were going to get the money, my husband and I filled out the card saying we'd give X amount of dollars over time to help our church grow.

What were we thinking? Heaven only knew. Ha, ha. When my husband went to work the following week he found out that he had been given a significant raise. We were given the means to meet our goal. Hallelujah. God provided for our need.

It was such an awesome step in faith and answer to our prayers. Our minister asked us to share our story with the congregation, so we did.

Heavenly Father, it is so awesome to witness answered prayer. Thank you for helping our faith to grow and remain strong.

Song Thoughts

"'Ere you left your room this morning, did you think to pray?"

29 – Crying Happy Tears

> You keep track of all my sorrows. You have collected all
> my tears in your bottle. You have recorded each one in
> your book. (Psalm 56:8 NLT)

I flew to Ohio the last week of October to take care of my young grandson and his little sister. My daughter and her husband traveled to the state of Oregon for his niece's wedding.

My grandson went to school every day, and my grand-daughter went to preschool for a few hours each morning. Several times we talked and shared pictures with their parents via texting. We counted the days until Halloween which would be the day after mommy and daddy returned.

When her parents returned, my granddaughter hugged her mom and burst into tears. She was embarrassed and did not want me to see that she was crying. I quickly told her that it was okay to cry because they were 'happy tears'.

Later, feeling much better, I overheard her proudly telling her friend that she had cried happy tears.

Thank you, Heavenly Father, for watching over us in times of sorrow, collecting our tears, and helping us to endure hardships.

Song Thoughts

"'Cause you're worth every falling tear, you're worth facing any fear.
But giving you all of me is where I'll start."

30–Who Knew?

Jesus looked at them and said, "With man this is impossible, but with God all things are possible." (Matthew 19:26 NIV)

Since I have MS, walking and simply having energy is challenging for me. Numerous times I have wished once again to have strong legs and good balance. If I could just have half the energy of a little child I'd be thrilled.

It can be easy to dwell on my problems, and forget the countless other blessings that God has given me out of the goodness of his heart. I have so very many.

One day I hurt the index finger on my left hand. It was badly bruised and sensitive to touch. Throughout the day, I was surprised at how many things I tried to do that hurt my finger. Tying my shoes was painful, as was turning a door knob, and even trying to blow my nose.

When my finger hurt as I went to pull on my sock the next morning, I paused to think how magnificent our bodies really are. God knew exactly what we needed when he created us. He knew we needed two hands and ten fingers. And what about two feet and ten toes, two eyes, two ears, and so on...

Omnipotent Father, we praise your name and thank you that we are fearfully and wonderfully made. Our bodies are so amazing.

Song Thoughts

"You raise me up, so I can stand on mountains,
you raise me up to walk on stormy seas."

31—Go Above and Beyond

> Whatever you do, work at it with all your heart,
> as working for the Lord, not for human masters.
> (Colossians 3:23 NIV)

A Wendy's fast food restaurant opened a few miles from us. My two teenage children got part-time jobs there.

When he found out that I ran a daycare in my home, the manager at <u>Wendy's</u> asked me to watch his little boy. It worked well for all of us.

Ordinarily the mom picked up their son, but one day I opened the door to his dad. He immediately said, "Yes, I'm here to pick up Davey, but I wanted to give you a compliment, too."

"Your son and daughter are the best employees ever. Not only do they show up when they're scheduled to work, they actually work when they get here! Your kids go above and beyond their job requirements. They do a lot of extra things that need to be done without even being asked. You should be a very proud mama."

Heavenly Father, we always want to have a serving heart for helping others. Thank you for the opportunities we have to show love.

Song Thoughts

"You call me out upon the waters, the great unknown
where feet may fail, and there I find you in the mystery."

32—Drawing Others to God

> He said to them, "Go into all the world and preach the
> gospel to all creation. (Mark 16:15 NIV)

Years ago several of us from our Bible Study small group went to a Halloween party together. My husband was a pirate and I dressed as a witch. One of our friends came up with an angel costume, thinking of church.

My daughter recently came across the nun habit she'd worn for the party, and decided she'd wear it to pass out treats to the neighborhood kids. When one little girl saw my daughter's costume, she asked, "Do you go to church?"

"Yes, I do," replied my daughter. "Do you?"

The little girl shook her head and sadly said, "No."

Running up to the door, a young boy trick-or-treating laughingly said, "I was going to ask for a treat, but I can see you have nun."

He immediately said, "Sorry, bad joke." We actually thought he was pretty clever and laughed.

Father, we pray that the things we say and do will draw others to you. We want to be a light in the world for you.

Song Thoughts

"There are souls to rescue, there are souls to save.
Send the light, send the light."

33—Be Kind to Everyone

> Do not repay evil with evil or insult with insult. On the contrary, repay evil with blessing, because to this you were called so that you may inherit a blessing. (1 Peter 3:9 NIV)

My parents had invited a bunch of our family friends to come over for an evening of food and fun. Mom made her special rotisserie chicken, and people brought pizzas as well as other yummy things to eat.

Knowing our family loved singing, several people even brought their guitars. We had a wonderful time singing and laughing together. Even so, we younger children were getting tired.

One friend loved my sister's blond curls and always teased her about them. That evening when he brought up her golden locks, deciding she'd had more than enough of his jokes about her hair, she responded rudely. My mother immediately sent my sister to her bedroom.

As people left, my sister kept watch from the upstairs window. When she saw her teasing friend walking to his car, she yelled, "And I meant it, too."

Forgive us, Lord, when we fall short of your will for our lives. Help us to look for the good in others as well as the best in all situations.

Song Thoughts

"You are good, you are good when there's nothing good in me, you are hope, you are hope you have covered all my sin."

34—Favorite Friends

> Then Peter began to speak: "I now realize how true it
> is that God does not show favoritism but accepts from
> every nation the one who fears him and does what is
> right." (Acts 10:34–35 NIV)

My family had a long time black friend named Cippio. He was very
special to us. My four year old son loved that Cippio always had
time to spend a few minutes with him when he stopped by for a visit. He
was like a good buddy. When they saw each other, they shared high 5's.

My son's favorite toy at Grandma's house was a mini bus that held
five or six little characters from Sesame Street. He would load up the
people and drive them on a tour around the rooms of Grandma's house.

One afternoon my mom and I watched, listening as he talked to
them. Bert, Ernie, Big Bird and the others were lined up for their ride. As
my son walked each person up the steps to their seat, we saw him pick up
the little black one and say, "Hop on the bus, Cippio." We had to laugh.

Dearest Lord, we want to love like little children. Help us to look at
other's hearts and not judge by their outward appearance

Song Thoughts

"Open the eyes of my heart, Lord, open the eyes of my heart,
I want to see you."

35—Soaking Up Sunshine

> His feet were like bronze glowing in a furnace, and his
> voice was like the sound of rushing waters. (Revelation
> 1:15 NIV)

We lived near ball fields and tennis courts. The town park also had swings, see-saws, sliding boards, monkey bars, and more.

There were always plenty of things to do. My kids loved playing outside on hot summer days and had the suntans to prove it.

My youngest daughter really tanned easily, and I teasingly told her that she was getting so dark people would think she lived down the street.

Our black friend asked, "Who lives down the street?"

My daughter quickly replied, "No one, no one at all."

Later after our friend left, I asked my daughter why she wouldn't tell him about the friendly black couple and their children who lived down the street.

My daughter replied, "I didn't want to make him feel funny."

Thank you, Lord, for giving us wisdom as we grow. Please help us to be kind to others and to love them as you love us.

Song Thoughts

"I'll sing for joy at the work of your hands,
forever I'll love you, forever I'll stand."

36—Always Beside Us

> Have I not commanded you? "Be strong and courageous.
> Do not be afraid; do not be discouraged, for the Lord
> your God will be with you wherever you go." (Joshua
> 1:9 NIV)

When I was diagnosed with MS in 1978 my symptom was numbness in my left hand. Eleven years later, the neurologist found lesions on my brain and suggested I use an Avonex injection once a week to slow down the progression of my Multiple Sclerosis. I was sick the entire day following each shot.

After five years of shots, I started feeling sick for two days, so I asked my neurologist, "If Avonex is supposed to make me feel better, why am I feeling worse?"

My neurologist suggested I stop the Avonex and try Tysabri. It was something new on the market. I sent the required insurance papers to my doctor via mail but he never received them. I tried a fax, but it never reached his office either. We repeated both, mail and fax, so they would have the necessary papers, but they still never made it to the doctor's office. How strange.

Then my doctor called to tell us that someone trying Tysabri had died. They temporarily took the drug off the market. Obviously, I wasn't meant to try it. God was watching over me.

So many times we forget that you are with us every moment of every day, even answering prayers we haven't thought to utter. Thank you, Lord.

Song Thoughts

"Your glory Lord is what our hearts long for, to be overcome by your presence Lord. Let us become more aware of your presence."

37–A Heart for Animals

> Be sure you know the condition of your flocks, give careful attention to your herds. (Proverbs 27:23 NIV)

My daughter was looking for a part-time job she would enjoy doing, preferably one that paid well. Loving animals, my daughter applied for a job at a pet clinic.

"How do you feel about euthanizing animals? Would you be able to do that?" asked the vet.

My daughter thought for a moment and in all honesty replied, "I don't know what that is, but I'm willing to learn. I'm sure I wouldn't have trouble doing it."

When my daughter got home, her sister and I asked how the interview had gone.

"I think it went well," she said, and enquired what euthanizing animals meant.

After we explained what it was, my daughter said with horror, "I sure hope they don't call and offer me the job. I could never do that."

Dear Father, help us to seek knowledge and make wise decisions. Guide us in each step we take.

Song Thoughts

"Christ alone, Cornerstone, weak made strong
in the Savior's love. He is Lord of all."

> But if serving the Lord seems undesirable to you, then
> choose for yourselves this day whom you will serve. But
> as for me and my household, we will serve the Lord."
> (Joshua 24:15 NIV)

We always enjoy spending a few days with our friends in Ft. Myers, Florida. They are wonderful hosts and tour guides. Their doors are always open to friends, yet they make me feel like family.

One time I basked and baked at Bonita Beach while my friend's husband helped my daughter build a really cool sandcastle. Some people were brave enough to get into the cool gulf waters, but I quickly retreated to a lounge chair with my friend after a quick toe-test and a shudder.

Afterwards, we were treated to the biggest ice cream cones I have ever seen, let alone eaten. Yum. yum!

We toured Thomas Edison's winter retreat together. In his lab these words were framed on the wall: "I have never failed. I've only found 10,000 ways that won't work."

I love his positive attitude.

Thank you, Lord for the blessing of so many friends in addition to our big family. We can only imagine how glorious heaven will be.

Song Thoughts

"Shout to the Lord all the earth let us sing
glory and majesty, praise to our King."

39—Get Out of the Boat

> Let the morning bring me word of your unfailing love, for I have put my trust in you. Show me the way I should go, for to you I entrust my life. (Psalm 143:8 NIV)

We took our daughter to the Virgin Islands for her 21ˢᵗ birthday. We all loved it. My husband joked that when he retired he'd buy a boat, and we could live there on the water.

For my birthday my daughter bought me a really cute little wooden boat. She said it reminded her of our trip.

My devotion that morning was taken from Matthew 14:28 NIV where Peter says, "Lord, if it's you, tell me to come to you on the water."

I had been indecisive about a choice I needed to make. Should I take the easier route or step out in faith? Seeing the boat, and remembering my devotions, brought tears to my eyes. I'm pretty sure God was giving me my answer.

Father, we thank you and praise you for answered prayer. Please help us to always seek your guidance.

Song Thoughts

"So remember your people, remember your children, remember your promise, oh God."

40—Making Mistakes

The Lord will keep you from all harm—he will watch over your life; the Lord will watch over your coming and going both now and forever more. (Psalm 121:8 NIV)

My two youngest sisters got ready for school. Grabbing their coats, they headed out to catch the school bus. When no one else was waiting at the stop, my sisters decided that they'd missed the bus. Our house rule was, if you missed the bus, you walked to school, about a mile away. Our parents had already left for work.

Freezing cold in their dresses, with bare legs exposed to the wind, they were finally almost there. A family friend we knew pulled to the curb. She asked why they were even outside, since due to inclement weather the schools had been closed. Really?

Our friend offered them a ride home, and they gladly accepted, not knowing whether to laugh or cry.

So often we fail to make wise decisions. Thank you for watching over us and sending others to help us.

Song Thoughts

"He's my friend, He's my Lord. Oh how I love Him, He's my Father."

41—Obey Our Parents

> Whoever spares the rod hates their children, but the one who loves their children is careful to discipline them. (Proverbs 13:24 NIV)

When my younger sister was born she only weighed about seven pounds. The rest of us started in the eight pound category. My sister often seemed to get bloody noses, so she was always given a little more special attention than the rest of us.

When and if my younger sister did get a spanking, she held on to daddy's hand. Then, they went in circles while she spanked him, too.

I actually don't remember getting many spankings, but I'm sure there were a few. When I turned thirteen, I happened to read an article that said, "Once children are thirteen years old, they should not get spankings anymore." That was great news.

One afternoon, just because I thought I would not get a spanking, I disobeyed my mom and dad. Uh oh... Surprise! They had obviously not read that article. Ouch.

Heavenly Father, please help us raise our children to walk according to your footsteps. Please help us all to be obedient in following you.

Song Thoughts

"Trust and obey, for there's no other way to be happy in Jesus."

42—Surprise, Surprise

> So in everything, do to others what you would have
> them do to you, for this sums up the Law and the
> Prophets. (Matthew 7:12 NIV)

Since I enjoyed meeting new people, I volunteered to be a greeter at our church. It was a quarterly position. Someone else would take a turn the next few months.

One Sunday morning, while standing at the front door welcoming people, I was pleased to meet a member of the Ohio State football coaching staff. He and his wife, along with their two children, were attending our church for the first time.

I kindly escorted their son and daughter to their Bible School classes. After the worship service, we said goodbye. I made the comment that I hoped they had enjoyed everything, and would come again next Sunday.

The following week they returned. They thanked me for being so nice to them on their first visit and handed me a ticket for the next OSU football game. My seat would be on the fifty yard line with the coaches' wives. How cool was that? Woo hoo!

Please help us, Father, to treat others the way we would like to be treated. Help us to always be kind to others without expecting anything in return.

Song Thoughts

"Rejoice in the Lord always, and again I say rejoice. Rejoice, rejoice."

43–Showing Love and Concern

> As a prisoner for the Lord, then, I urge you to live a life worthy of the calling you have received. Be completely humble and gentle; be patient, bearing with one another in love. (Ephesians 4:1–2 NIV)

My neighbor lady, a few doors down, and I became good friends. One winter she gave my daughter and me some free tickets to go see Charles Dickens <u>A Christmas Carol</u>. Then another time she gave us tickets so that we could go watch <u>Disney on Ice</u>. Both were fun events.

We'd occasionally go shopping at the mall or to garage sales together. We attended different churches, but sometimes we shared our faith with each other.

As my daily walking buddy, she began to notice that I often stubbed my toe as we headed down the sidewalk. With concern about me falling, she suggested that I might want to talk to my neurologist to see if there were any changes with my MS.

Dear heavenly Father, sometimes we tend to ignore problems, and sometimes we don't even notice. Thank you for the friends and loved ones that care about us.

Song Thoughts

"Prone to wander, Lord, I feel it. Here's my heart, oh, take and seal it. Seal it for thy courts above."

44–Have a Great Time

> We then who are strong ought to bear the infirmities
> of the weak, and not to please ourselves. (Romans
> 15:1 KJV)

Our younger children's church youth group was having a skating party at the Ohio State University Ice Rink. My daughter was excited to go, even though she'd never been on skates.

That Sunday I asked a couple of people in my Bible school class about helping my daughter learn to ice skate. Since I knew they loved skating, I thought they might enjoy the opportunity to go for free. A new guy, Michael, who had only come to our class for a few weeks volunteered to meet us there.

My daughter and I arrived a little early and waited in the parking lot for awhile. When we got tired of being outside, we entered the rental area, and I helped her put on some skates.

Still not seeing Michael, I told my daughter that she would just have to try skating alone. She agreed, and we went into the ice rink area. There was Michael, with his skates on, patiently waiting. I'm not sure who had more fun.

We have so many blessings, Lord. Please help us to always be willing to reach out and help others.

Song Thoughts

"When Jesus shows his smiling face, there is sunshine in my soul."

45—Jesus Is Lord

> For God so loved the world that he gave his one and
> only Son, that whoever believes in him shall not perish
> but have eternal life. (John 3:16 NIV)

I pretty much spent every Sunday evening with our church youth
group. Each Saturday morning was spent at junior choir practices.
On Sundays we always went to the worship services at church, as well
as Bible school classes. Wednesday evenings were for Bible studies.

Sometimes our church held services every evening for an entire week.
Revival services were held to encourage all the believers. Evangelistic
services reached out to unbelievers.

After listening to an evangelistic speaker, I made the decision to
publicly acknowledge my faith. When we stood to sing the invitation
hymn, I felt the urge to walk forward and make the good confession.
I was scared, hanging on tightly to the back of the pew. My heart said
let go, so I did, and walked up front to proclaim Jesus as my Lord and
Savior. I was then baptized.

Thank you, Father, for sending Jesus, your only Son to pay for our
sins. Thank you, Jesus, for dying on the cross for us. We're so unworthy
of your love.

Song Thoughts

"In my Father's house there's a place for me,
I'm a Child of God. Yes I am."

46—Open My Eyes

> "What do you want me to do for you?" Jesus asked him. The blind man said, "Rabbi, I want to see." "Go," said Jesus, "your faith has healed you." Immediately he received his sight and followed Jesus along the road. (Mark 10:51–52 NIV)

I've always loved babies. Babies seem like a gift, fresh from heaven. My mom liked babies, too. One Sunday, my mom agreed to watch her friend's baby the following day. I was excited, but unfortunately, I'd have to attend school. Phooey.

The next morning when I woke up, it felt like my eyes were glued shut. Since I had just heard the story of a blind man asking Jesus to restore his sight, I panicked. I ran down the hall screaming and crying, "I'm blind."

Comforting me, my mom explained that my eyes were only matted shut. She said that I probably had pink eye.

I didn't have to attend school, and I was home when the baby came, even though I couldn't touch him. Instead, I had to visit the doctor for a prescription. Doggone it.

Heavenly Father, we take our blessings for granted and so often forget to praise you. Thank you so much for everything you give us, not just food and clothes, but also for our amazing bodies.

Song Thoughts

"Fear is losing ground to our hope in you.
Unstoppable God, let your glory go on and on."

47–Singing For Joy

> Sing to him, sing praise to him; tell of all his wonderful acts. Glory in his holy name; let the hearts of those who seek the Lord rejoice. (Psalm 105:2–3 NIV)

I've sung many songs to my children and grandchildren. Beginning a long time ago, I sang songs to my children when they were babies. As they got older, the kids would ask me to sing to them after they hopped into bed. We all loved it.

When we visit our grandchildren the days always pass quickly, and soon it is bedtime. After getting baths and putting on pajamas, they drag their feet about brushing their teeth and crawling into bed.

Somewhere along the line, their dad or mom started saying, "If you hurry and brush your teeth, Nanny might sing some songs for you."

That always speeded things up, and soon all was quiet, except for me singing songs. I enjoy it just as much as they do. I think about the memories they will have to cherish one day.

Thank you, heavenly Father, for the gift of singing. Let our voices always bring praises to your name and joy to our hearts.

Song Thoughts

"Good night, our God is watching o'er you, His blessings go before you, I'll be praying for you. God bless you."

48—Fun Together

Children's children are a crown to the aged, and parents
are the pride of their children. (Proverbs 17:6 NIV)

Many of my grandsons are now taller than me. Some are as tall as
granddaddy, over six feet! They are all good-looking, smart, very
talented, and athletic. I could go on and on.

It thrilled my heart one Sunday morning to observe two of my
grandsons serving communion and taking up the offering at church
when we were visiting. The youth group guys were ushers that day.

I was also tickled to be part of a special girl time as my beautiful
granddaughter got ready for the homecoming dance. I had almost
forgotten about all those fun things we girls enjoyed such as getting our
hair arranged elegantly, and having our fingernails professionally done.
Wearing make-up and buying jewelry, as well as finding the perfect dress,
were all part of preparing for this special evening.

Thank you, Father for loving us and for all the extra fun things that
brighten our lives each day. Your blessings never end.

Song Thoughts

"When He shall come with trumpet sound,
oh, may I then in him be found;
dressed in His righteousness alone, faultless stand before the throne."

49—*Love Is Patient*

> Above all, love each other deeply, because love covers over a multitude of sins. Offer hospitality to one another without grumbling. (1 Peter 4:8–9 NIV)

Our church joined forces with another congregation. Their pastor's wife volunteered to be the full time accompanist for our church choir.

At one of the first practices, our director was having a bad day. The pianist, actually everyone, was unfamiliar with the song he wanted us to sing. The choir director was very frustrated.

Usually a really nice man, patience was not his strong suit that evening. He kept stomping over to the piano, to pound out the way he felt it should be. I felt that our new volunteer bore the brunt of his dissatisfaction. My heart went out to our pianist.

When I got home that evening, I wrote her a brief note of encouragement. I simply told her that I was happy she was now part of our choir and how very tickled we were to have her.

The next week at choir practice she sought me out. She wanted to tell me how much she appreciated my thoughtfulness and encouragement.

Dear Lord, please help us to always go the extra mile in showing kindness to others. It's so easy to think only of ourselves and forget about others.

Song Thoughts

"Do not wait until a deed of kindness you may do,
brighten the corner where you are."

50–I Can't Remember

"For behold, I create new heavens and a new earth;
And the former shall not be remembered or come to
mind. (Isaiah 65:17 NKJV)

As I sat in church listening to the sermon, I heard the pastor say, "Your brain contains more than 100 billion nerve cells. Each cell is connected to 10,000 other neurons. You are talking to yourself right now. Research indicates most people speak at a rate of 150 to 200 words per minute, but the internal dialogue, which means talking to yourself, is more like 1,300 words per minute."

Yikes! Just hearing something like that is mind boggling. I walked out of the building thinking about what had been said. No wonder it's so hard to remember everything. My mind must be on overload. That is certainly a lot of information.

Even so, it reminds me of something I once heard. Not everything can be answered by the brain. Sometimes you have to use your heart.

Later that afternoon when we were back at our home, I walked from the living room into my bedroom. Now why did I come in here?

Heavenly Father, you have created many beautiful wonders. Our minds and our bodies are simply amazing. You are awesome, Lord.

Song Thoughts

"Who can grasp your infinite wisdom? Holy God,
to whom all praise is due I stand in awe of you."

51—All God's Children

> Ye are of God, little children, and have overcome them: because greater is he that is in you, than he that is in the world. (1 John 4:4 KJV)

My three-year-old granddaughter is constantly telling her mother, "I want to go see my Nanny and ride in Nanny's car."

My little grandson's favorite sweatshirt reads, "Who needs Santa, I've got Grandma!"

She eventually adjusted to second grade and her twenty-five year old male teacher, who looked like he might be sixteen years old. He said, "She's an excellent, well-rounded student, and I really enjoy having her in class."

She said, "I didn't want a boy teacher! He's very nice, and I like him a lot, but it's just not me!"

After three months she loved having a boy teacher, could hardly wait to get to school, never wanted to miss or leave early, and made many new friends.

Heavenly Father, each day is such a blessing. You know our needs. You give us so many things to brighten our lives. We praise you and give you our thanks.

Song Thoughts

"Forever He is glorified, forever He is lifted high.
We sing hallelujah. The Lamb has overcome."

> In everything I did, I showed you that by this kind of hard work we must help the weak, remembering the words the Lord Jesus himself said: "It is more blessed to give than to receive." (Acts 20:35 NIV)

While still in high school, two of my daughters were blessed to go on a mission trip. They went with a group of teens and adults from our church to Tijuana.

In Mexico, they helped build houses with two-by-fours and chicken wire. Each home had only one door and one window. My daughter found a talent she did not know existed. She excelled at putting stucco on the walls. LOL.

The recipients of the homes were thrilled. Having a house to live in was a dream come true for them. Even their little kids were tickled, giggling excitedly.

What an invaluable learning experience for my daughters! When the girls got home, they exclaimed in amazement, "They don't have anything and yet they're so happy."

Thank you, Father, for the opportunities and talents that you have blessed us with. Please help us to always use those gifts to show love to others.

Song Thoughts

"Love, love, love, love, the gospel in a word is love.
Love thy neighbor as thy brother."

53—Pass It On

> Anyone who has been stealing must steal no longer,
> but must work, doing something useful with their own
> hands, that they may have something to share with
> those in need. (Ephesians 4:28 NIV)

Twenty-seven of my wonderful Christian friends, along with a few family members, helped move all our things into a new condo. Ten days later we were robbed.

Hoping to get a new couch, I had been saving any extra money to pay for my purchase. I kept the money in my wallet, carrying it around in my purse.

While out shopping for a couch, I succumbed to buying myself a new purse. Arriving home, I excitedly changed all my things from one purse to the other. We were tired and soon headed to bed.

Something woke me up in the wee hours. I wandered down the hall and saw the door leading to the garage standing wide open. My new purse was gone. So was all my money.

I called the police, but my purse and money were never recovered. Thankfully, God had been watching over us, and we were unharmed.

Some of my friends heard about the robbery. They came by to offer their love and support. One guy gave me fifty dollars. I tried refusing it, but he said, "Just pass it on to someone else once you're back on your feet."

Father, we're so thankful knowing that no matter where we go, you're always with us, guarding us and keeping us safe. Thank you also for the love and generosity of friends.

Song Thoughts

"Love lifted me, when nothing else could help, love lifted me."

54—God is Watching Over You

> "Forget the former things; do not dwell on the past.
> See I am doing a new thing! Now it springs up; do you
> not perceive it? I am making a way in the wilderness
> and streams in the wasteland. (Isaiah 43:18–19 NIV)

We lived in the Columbus, Ohio area. Graduating from high school, my daughter and her best friends wanted to take their first road trip without an adult chaperone. Feeling they were now fully grown, driving to Myrtle Beach, South Carolina, all by themselves sounded great.

We, moms especially, prayed a lot. They were going in a minivan, and the girls were taking turns driving. They promised to stay in touch and keep us updated.

The girls contacted us when they were lost somewhere in Pennsylvania. They had missed the correct exit and somehow ended up going the wrong way. South Carolina by way of Pennsylvania, need I say more?

Thankfully, we were able to figure out how they'd gone wrong and where they were. We were able to help them get back to the freeway, and once again heading in the southern direction. It was a miracle. LOL.

The girls eventually made it to South Carolina. They had a wonderful time at the beach, enjoying the sunshine, lying in the sand to tan, and taking an occasional swim.

I'm not sure if they took the scenic route again when returning to Ohio, but they eventually managed to find their way home safely. Hallelujah.

Even when we so often forget to say thanks, we're grateful, dear Lord, to know that you're always nearby, watching over us day and night. Thank you, too, Father, for your guidance.

Song Thoughts

"Keep on the right side, always on the right
side of the road. Oh glory hallelujah."

55–Asking in Faith

> If you believe, you will receive whatever you ask for in
> prayer." (Matthew 21:23 NIV)

As we closed our Women's Bible study session, I prayed, "Lord, you know how lonely I have been. If there is someone out there for me, please bring him into my life. If not, please fill my emptiness with you."

Shortly thereafter, I met a wonderful Christian man. Dr. Zoeller did physics research for Ohio State University. Michael came to church with our mutual friend, an OSU Physics Professor. Professor Pennington had recently started coming to church. I met him one Sunday when he actually had the nerve to sit in my pew. Ha, ha.

Later that year, Michael proposed to me, and we were married in December. We both feel that God brought us together.

I found myself telling my friends, "I can't even begin to tell you how very special he is to me. It seems like a wonderful dream, and I have to keep pinching myself to make sure it's real."

Michael and my little girl got along great with their fun-loving personalities, silliness, and jokes. He taught her how to ice skate. I can't tell who enjoyed it more. Perhaps it was me, just watching them. Guess what Santa brought for Christmas that year?

Praise your name, Father. We often forget to ask for your help. We thank you for hearing us and answering our prayers, often above and beyond our expectations.

Song Thoughts

"Nothing shall be impossible, your kingdom reigns unstoppable.
Let your glory go on and on."

56–Teaching and Training

> All Scripture is God-breathed and is useful for teaching, rebuking, correcting and training in righteousness, so that the servant of God may be thoroughly equipped for every good work. (2 Timothy 3:16–17 NIV)

I am a very proud mama of my little girl. She had a boy teacher for the second year in a row, but seemed to thoroughly enjoy school. She was an intelligent little girl with a memory like a sponge. It served her well.

She played Bible Bowl which entailed studying different books of the Bible and memorizing scripture. Questions about various parables and teachings were also asked. She always scored in first or second place when taking the written exam for each competition.

When my daughter asked me to teach her how, I showed her the way to braid the Barbie dolls' hair. She loved giving all her dolls new hair-dos.

She continued dancing ballet and participating in Girl Scouts, as well as singing in the children's choir at church. She still loves doing many things, especially hair, but like her mom, I think that reading just might be one of her favorite pastimes, too.

Blessing after blessing, you give us throughout our lives. Thank you, Father, for your loving kindness and for giving us talents and wisdom along with numerous blessings.

Song Thoughts

"Praise the Lord, praise the Lord, let the earth hear his voice,
Praise the Lord, let the people rejoice."

57—Friends of My Heart

Just as lotions and fragrance give sensual delight, a sweet friendship refreshes the soul. (Proverbs 27:9 MSG)

Shortly after our move, we invited the minister and his wife for dinner. She volunteered to help clean-up and started scraping food off the plates into the disposal. She didn't know it didn't work. She felt terrible, but we ended up laughing together and became good friends.

When her sons had football practice and couldn't do their part-time jobs, I helped her clean some offices for them. We even ironed brown paper bags on the church carpeting to remove wax left by dripping candles after the candlelight Christmas Eve service.

On Wednesday evenings, prior to Bible study and choir practice, we helped a few other people prepare meals for everyone. It worked perfectly for those who came straight from work or mothers who liked having a break from cooking.

On summer afternoons, we often took walks together around the neighborhood. We laughed and talked as much as we walked.

More times than I'd like to admit, we'd go someplace and accidentally lock the keys in the car. After coming to our rescue about half a dozen times, her husband said, "I'm not sure it's safe to allow you two to hang out together." LOL.

The blessing of Christian friends and fellow loved-ones are a significant part of our lives. Thank you, Father, for the path you lay before us.

Song Thoughts

"Walkin' on the heaven road, I'm gonna lay down my heavy load, 'cause Jesus said he'd walk along with me."

58—Count Blessings, Not Mistakes

> Study to show thyself approved unto God; a workman
> that needeth not to be ashamed, rightly dividing the
> word of truth. (2 Timothy 2:15 KJV)

My friend volunteered to lead our church's Bible Bowl team. I agreed to help her. We wrote questions for practices as well as competitions and helped the teens study. We drove to other churches in the area to compete. One of our strongest competitors was the church in Caldwell, Ohio.

The grand finale was at the North American Christian Convention held in different states each year. Teams from all over would come and compete against each other.

As we were flying to Oklahoma for the NACC, our plane had a layover in Kansas. Hearing the announce-ment that we would soon board the plane, we decided to make a quick trip to the ladies room.

When we returned, people were starting to board the plane. My friend, realizing she had left her purse hanging in the restroom, asked me to run and get it. When I ran back with her purse, she was standing there watching the doors of the walkway close. I quickly told the attendant standing there, that we were supposed to be on the plane. She responded, "It already left."

"No, it hasn't." I said. I could see through the window that the plane was still backing up.

She looked at me sadly, and said, "Honey, it's gone."

On a lighter note, our pastor here in New York is one of those Caldwell, Ohio, Bible Bowl boys. It's a small world.

Heavenly Father, so many times we fall short of your will for our lives, yet you continue to love us. Thank you for your leadership and direction.

Song Thoughts

"Sweet hour of prayer that calls me from a world of care.
In seasons of distress and grief, my soul has often found relief."

59—Bundles of Blessings

> The good man does not escape troubles-he has them,
> too. But the Lord helps him in each and every one.
> (Psalm 34:19 TLB)

My daughter was pregnant. Panicked, she called me to take her to the Emergency Room. The nurse said, "I'm sorry you lost a baby, but there's still two in there."

Surprise! The Obstetrician had not noticed my daughter was carrying triplets. She ended up having twins, a boy and a girl.

After the babies were born, I helped my daughter a lot. Living only a few miles away from her made it very easy. I often took care of the little girl, calling her my baby.

Like all newborns, they woke up for their regular feedings, burping, and diaper changes. One night, her little girl was more fussy than usual. Even daddy didn't have the magic touch.

I was awakened in the wee hours by the ringing of my phone. I answered it to hear my daughter wearily say, "You better come get your baby. She won't stop crying." I happily went to help.

About a year later, my daughter and I drove past a house displaying a huge sign in the front yard that said, "We have triplets."

Remembering the early chaotic days we looked at each other, laughing as we said, "Those poor people."

Heavenly Father, thank you for the children and grandchildren you give us to bless our lives. Thanks, too, for helping us through those more difficult times.

Song Thoughts

"And He will surely give you rest by trusting in His word.
Only trust Him, only trust Him."

> Instead, you ought to say, "If it is the Lord's will, we will live and do this or that." (James 4:15 NIV)

My husband is a very handy man. One day I asked him if there was anything he couldn't do. He wasn't able to think of anything. His talent is extremely helpful to our kids and I don't believe they ever hesitate to ask him for assistance. Maybe that's why we live in New York, and they all live in Ohio, so he can get some rest. Tee Hee.

One Saturday while we were in Ohio, he was helping to put up a new backsplash. My daughter, her husband, and their two youngest children had to leave for an appointment with their dentist for a check-up and to have their teeth cleaned. My granddaughter didn't want to leave me, but I assured her I'd still be there when they returned.

A couple hours later, four-year-old Janie excitedly ran into the house to tell me that she didn't have any cavities. She told me that the dentist said, "She had teeth like a princess."

Not quite so elated, yet happy, my grandson said he didn't have any cavities either. I asked, "Who did the dentist say you had teeth like? Ninja Turtles?"

It was just a guess, but my grandson got a big grin on his face. Do Ninja Turtles even have teeth? Oh wait, I think they grow vampire fangs.

Thank you so much for our numerous blessings. Thanks for all fourteen of my grandchildren. I never knew what joy they would bring to my life.

Song Thoughts

"There is a name I love to hear, the sweetest name on earth. It sounds like music in my ears. Oh, how I love Jesus."

61–Days Gone By

> Recalling your tears, I long to see you, so that I may
> be filled with joy. I am reminded of your sincere faith,
> which first lived in your grandmother Lois and in your
> mother Eunice and, I am persuaded now lives in you.
> (2 Timothy 1:4–5 NIV)

I never went to kindergarten. I don't even think I was in school. I was still pretty young yet some of my fondest memories are of being at my grandparent's farm.

Grandma churned cream into butter. Sometimes, I got to help turn the crank. Other times, she made smear case and cottage cheese on their back porch.

There was a springhouse where we went to get cold, fresh water to drink. Or we'd just go there to cool down.

They also had a chicken coop, sometimes called the hen house. I don't know why. It was fun to help gather eggs. Sprinkling grain for the chickens was pretty cool, too.

Grandpa let me ride along bareback, while he used the work horse to lift bales of hay up into the loft of the barn. Gee means go right. Haw means go left. That's horse talk.

My sisters and I spent plenty of time playing in the corn crib, when they weren't trying to teach us how to milk a cow. None of us ever quite got the knack of that.

As simple as it sounds, we loved having an enclosed hideaway under the weeping willow tree. It got a lot of use when we played hide-and-seek.

Heavenly Father, we have enjoyed many blessings. Thank you for those who passed their faith on to us. We look forward to seeing them again in heaven. Thanks, too, for modern conveniences.

Song Thoughts

"Wherever He leads I'll go. Wherever He leads I'll go.
I'll follow the one who loves me so."

62—Helping Others

> Each of you should use whatever gift you have received
> to serve others, as faithful stewards of God's grace in
> its various forms. (1 Peter 4:10 NIV)

My youngest daughter was growing up way too fast. I can clearly remember seeing her with shaving cream everywhere. She tried to shave her legs when she was only about two years old. Monkey see, monkey do. LOL.

Knowing I didn't want to miss a minute, once she was in school, I decided to accompany her class on some of their field trips. One educational trip we took, when she was in second grade, was to the Fire Department.

The firemen were really nice and loved showing us their truck and protective gear. Kids, especially the boys, were anxious to try on the big firemen coats. They had no idea how much they weighed.

After helping a student put his arms into the jacket, the fireman let go and quickly swooped behind the boy to catch him. It was so heavy he couldn't remain standing upright while wearing it.

I reached out to see if his coat was really that heavy. I could barely lift it. It definitely weighed a ton.

How can firemen move so quickly when they're grabbing hoses and running into burning buildings? That's not even including any axes or ladders they might be carrying.

Thank you so much for the brave men who use their talents to assist us and save the lives of so many people. Please help us to wisely use the gifts you give us, too.

Song Thoughts

"It's all about Him and the love that He gives, you can walk all alone, never find your way home, 'til you see deep within, it's all about Him."

63—*Sing, Sing, Sing*

> Come, let us sing for joy to the Lord; let us shout aloud
> to the Rock of our salvation. Let us come before him
> with thanksgiving and extol him with music and song.
> (Psalm 95:1–2 NIV)

My husband's employer really appreciates him. His colleagues like him a lot, too. Whenever I see any of them, they are very nice and friendly to me. Better yet, my husband loves his job. He gets paid well, and sometimes he is surprised by a nice bonus check.

My husband's company always has several events each year for their employees to enjoy. For example, they have shopping trips to NYC, tickets for the Tri-City Valley Cats minor baseball games, and picnics at the Saratoga Race track. My husband and I try to participate in most of the events.

In December, we attended the annual Christmas party at Proctor's Theatre, a former vaudeville house located in Schenectady, NY. They had a very nice dinner that included assorted choices of appetizers and desserts, along with several beverages.

The entertainment varies. They have had various quiz games, dancing, and karaoke. A few times, they've also had photo booths.

There were eight to ten people seated at each table last year. They gave each group a pen and a paper with lines from about twenty or so Christmas songs. We were to guess the title of each song by the words or clue given in that one line.

With my love of singing, I was pretty much familiar with all of the songs they were referring to. Our table won a gift card for Target. The guys kindly handed it to me with a smile, saying I knew the most answers. I haven't spent it yet.

We thank you Father for fun times with friends. Thank you also for good food and the multiple blessings that you give us throughout our lives.

Song Thoughts

"Holy, holy is the Lord God Almighty who was and is, and is to come."

64—You Gotta Love 'Em

> The wolf will live with the lamb, the leopard will lie down with the goat, the calf and the lion and the yearling together; and a little child shall lead them. (Isaiah 11:6 NIV)

My husband and I love the fall, especially when it's harvest time again. We enjoy going to the local Farmers' Market to buy fresh vegetables.

One Saturday morning, we headed out to buy some corn on the cob and tomatoes, along with anything else that looked good. When we arrived at the booths, we noticed that a truck from the Humane Society was there. They had set up a fenced-in area for kittens and puppies. They were so adorable. We could not walk by without stopping to pet them.

Checking out the various tents, we found the veggies we wanted. Purchasing our food, we headed back toward the parking lot. As we walked by the fenced area, we saw that only one, lonely, little, orange kitty was left. She was all by herself. She looked at us with soulful eyes.

Needless to say, we came home with corn, tomatoes, zucchini and a new pet. We call our youngest daughter Sugar Bear, so we named the newest member of our family Honey Bear. I'm not sure how it happened, but she is now queen of the household.

Thank you, heavenly Father for animals, and the affection that we feel for them. You so generously give us many things to brighten and bless our lives.

Song Thoughts

"The animals are coming one by one the old
cow chewing on a caraway bun.
There's animals and animals and animals and
animals and animals and animals, yes, Lord."

65—Give Help

For we are God's handiwork, created in Christ Jesus to
do good works, which God prepared in advance for us
to do. (Ephesians 2:10 NIV)

My daughter loved Girl Scouts. She and the troop leader's daughter
were best friends. It was nice that the girls attended the same school
and lived almost next door to each other.

The Troop leader and I became friends, too. I tried to assist and
help whenever I could. When the time for Girl Scout cookie sales
rolled around, I volunteered to head the project. I'm not sure what I was
thinking. Ha, ha.

The girls were young, energetic, and excited. Cookie sales were
phenomenal. When the delivery truck driver unloaded over two hundred
and fifty boxes of Girl Scout cookies into my garage, I could only stand
back, and watch in amazement. Yikes!

Thankfully, all went well, and I got the right boxes to each child.
The girls got the cookies delivered to the correct buyers and collected
the money.

When Girl Scout cookie time arrived the following year, I hoped
someone else would step up to be in charge, but that never happened. No
one told me that I had signed up for a lifetime position. Who knew? LOL.

Heavenly Father, we know that our loads get lighter when we work
together and help each other. Thank you for willing hearts.

Song Thoughts

"When all my labors and trials are o'er, just to be near
the dear Lord I adore, that will be glory for me."

66—All God's Creatures

Look at the birds of the air, for they neither sow nor reap nor gather into barns; yet your heavenly Father feeds them. Are you not of more value than they? (Matthew 6:26 NKJV)

We returned to New York after living in Wisconsin for seven years. Yes, my heart is in Ohio, but I left a small piece of it in Wisconsin with our Bible study small group friends. I miss some things about that house and our neighbors there, too. Moving isn't easy.

Shortly after our move, as we were getting settled, we looked out the window. There between our house and the neighbor's house were four wild turkeys. Suddenly, one turkey started loping across the backyard. Then, we saw a turtle, bigger than a dinner plate, slowly moving through the grass beside the turkey. My husband grabbed his phone and took a video of their trek. I can't really call it a race, but it did make me think of the tortoise and the hare.

That night our motion detector light came on in our back yard. When we opened the blinds to look, we saw five small deer, staring right back at us.

A couple days later, I went outside to sit and relax on our back porch for awhile. I was amazed to see all the animals running everywhere. With nothing better to do I started naming them. Chip and Dale, Peter Rabbit, Gray Squirrel, his brother Brown Squirrel, and I can't forget Bambi and her friends, plus Pokey the turtle, along with Tom Turkey and his buddies.

There are so many joys just seeing the little critters you created and knowing that they are all loved by you and are part of your plan. Thank you, Lord.

Song Thoughts

"All God's creatures got a place in the choir. Some sing low and some sing higher. Some just clap their hands."

67—Fondly Remembering

> Love is patient, love is kind. It does not envy, it does not boast, it is not proud. It does not dishonor others, it is not self-seeking, it is not easily angered, it keeps no record of wrongs. Love does not delight in evil but rejoices with the truth. It always protects, always trusts, always hopes, always perseveres. (1 Corinthians 13:4–7 NIV)

I've been thinking of my children, and remembering the days gone by. The love, laughter and memories we share are very special, bringing smiles to my face.

I was browsing through the three books that my youngest daughter made for me when she was in elementary school. They are priceless keepsakes.

She wrote about learning to dance at her sister's wedding. We have a picture of her dancing, her head barely coming up to his shoulder, as my son-in-law's brother gave her instructions about moving her feet.

Annie's pictures and stories helped us remember the excitement and laughter the day her brother was married. She got to be the flower girl. My oldest grandson, actually my only grandson at that time, was the ring bearer. He was in his terrible two's.

As she scattered the rose petals down the aisle, Tommy, carrying the pillow with the rings on it, followed after her. Each time she stretched out her hand, and a petal fluttered to the floor, he quickly stomped on it.

Thank you, Father, for our families; the fun and the joy they bring into our hearts and the memories we have made along the way.

Song Thoughts

"Give me one glorious ambition for my life, Lord, to know and follow hard after you. Lead me on and I will run after you."

He said, "Throw your net on the right side of the boat and you will find some." When they did, they were unable to haul the net in because of the large number of fish. (John 21:6 NIV)

We visited my sister and her husband in Homer, Alaska. Their address was actually Anchor Point, AK. August was a pleasant time of year to go, with daily temperatures mostly being sixty-five to seventy-five degrees. We saw a few people swimming. Brrr...

The day we went to a fishing place called The Spit, we wore jackets. Michael had to put on waders. He was tickled with his borrowed gear, and held up his fishing rod saying, "See my fishing stick?" Laughing, my brother-in-law rolled his eyes, but the pole was actually called an Ugly Stick.

Some guys complained about Michael having a bobber, not knowing he wasn't a seasoned fisherman. We did our best to ignore them.

After a short time, Michael said he felt something pulling on his pole. Following instructions, he played the line and eventually reeled in a twenty-seven pound King Salmon. Ta dah. Talk about first time luck.

Thank you, Father, for the blessings you give us. Please help us to become fishers of men, drawing others to you.

Song Thoughts

"Hear Christ calling come unto me, come unto me.
I will make you fishers of men if you follow me."

69–We All Make Mistakes

> He does not treat us as our sins deserve or repay us according to our iniquities. For as high as the heavens are above the earth, so great is his love for those who fear him; as far as the east is from the west, so far has he removed our transgressions from us. (Psalm 103:10–12 NIV)

Grandma moved in with us. Not having any other space, my mom made grandma a bedroom in our sunroom. Since the room had a wall of windows on three sides, there was usually a nice cool breeze on warm summer nights. My sisters and I liked to take turns sleeping with grandma.

Grandma taught me how to make real 'honest to goodness' lemonade! First, you roll a lemon to soften it, then cut it in half and use a juicer to squeeze out the juice. Then you add sugar and water. Tah dah. It was the best lemonade ever. I almost drank the whole pitcher by myself.

It was my night to sleep with grandma. The next morning when I woke up, I was soaking wet.

"Mom," I yelled. "Grandma wet the bed."

"Hmmm...?" Grandma said. "My nightgown is dry."

Father, so many times we make mistakes and often fall short of your will. Thank you for your mercy, and for always forgiving us.

Song Thoughts

"Would you be free from your burden of sin, there's power in the blood. There's wonderful power in the blood."

> Don't let anyone look down on you because you are young, but set an example for the believers in speech, in conduct, in love, in faith and in purity. (1 Timothy 4:12 NIV)

My son has a good heart. He's quite outgoing. He especially enjoys sports and is very athletic. He was a good student academically, too. He's always had tons of friends.

I remember joining the excited bunch of kids when our church youth group and their families went on their very first snow skiing trip to Mad River Mountain. Being a novice, I stuck to the bunny slope that was made for beginners. My son, on the other hand, took off on his skis like a pro.

I will never forget the time I went to the fifth grade parent/teacher conference for my son's class. His teacher greeted me with a big smile. He was anxious to tell me about a short quiz he had given the students. Just for the fun of it, question number ten asked, "Who would you want to be if you had a chance to be someone else?"

The teacher thought some of the kids might give an answer such as wanting to be the President of the United States. Nope. Every boy in my son's class said they wanted to be HIM, my son.

Thank you, Lord, for the guidance you give us as we raise our children. Help us to always be available to them as you are to us every moment as well as in times of need.

Song Thoughts

"You were the Word at the beginning, one
with God the Lord Most High.
Yours is the kingdom, yours is the glory."

71—Riches in Heaven

> But as it is written: "Eye has not seen, nor ear heard, nor have entered into the heart of man the things which God has prepared for those who love Him." (1 Corinthians 2:9 NKJV)

Having three girls in our family, we accumulated a few Barbie dolls over the years. Okay, we had a whole bunch of them. Our youngest daughter moved to New York with us for awhile before deciding to return to Ohio to live nearer her siblings. She knew we'd move back there eventually.

I'd sorted through childhood things belonging to the three older kids prior to each move. Only our youngest daughter still has some things with daddy and mommy.

Our youngest granddaughter was anticipating a trip to Nanny's. Since I hadn't seen any, I told her that we didn't have any Barbie dolls.

"Yes, you do." Ann told me. "Mine are still there."

Her dad checked the closet. "I started counting them, but didn't want to waste time." He told me.

"You're right. Daddy found your Barbie dolls. He figures there are about thirty eight of them." I told my daughter.

"I counted them as I put them into the box. There's sixty-six." She replied. "But, I'm not sure how many Ken and Chelsea dolls there might be."

"When are we going to Nanny's?" My granddaughter repeatedly questioned her mommy. "I want to see her hundred Barbie dolls."

Father, our blessings are so many, far more than we need. Thank you for all the little things in our lives that we often fail to appreciate and the joy they bring.

Song Thoughts

"Praise God from whom all blessings flow.
Praise Him all creatures here below."

> For the word of God is alive and active. Sharper than any double-edged sword, it penetrates even to dividing soul and spirit, joints and marrow; it judges the thoughts and attitudes of the heart. (Hebrews 4:12 NIV)

What did the Easter bunny bring you? Nothing yet, but my mom gave me these bracelets in my Easter basket.

I want to be a preacher when I grow up. Then I'll only have to work for one hour, one day a week on Sunday.

They said they are moving to Florida because there's no snow. How do people live without snow?

When I get older, I want to work at the Dairy Queen. When we're not busy, I'll just stick my mouth under that thing where the ice cream comes out instead of a cone.

Standing at the Sportsman's Club she asked, "When is it my turn?" lazily swinging the gun at her side.

She was impatiently waiting to try shooting a clay pigeon. She accidently pulled the trigger, shooting off a corner of the sidewalk. It flew up, hitting the guy beside her in the knee. Oops.

"She shot me." he yelled.

Nope, just a flying piece of cement that didn't even tear a hole in the leg of his pants, thank goodness.

Nevertheless, he had a crazy story to tell his friends. "And, watch out for those little Kula girls."

Heavenly Father, we thank you for continuing to guide us throughout our lives. Please help us to heed the path you set before us.

Song Thoughts

"Who, oh Lord, could save themselves?
You alone can rescue, you alone can save."

73—A Moment in Time

Let us not become weary in doing good, for at the
proper time we will reap a harvest if we do not give up.
(Galatians 6:9 NIV)

They were building a new housing development about a mile away from my mom. Since she no longer needed multiple bedrooms, not to mention all the extra space, she decided to sell our childhood home. She happily picked out the ranch floor plan she liked, excited to move into a new house.

After moving, Mom quickly made friends with her new neighbors. Dave, his wife, and their three teenage sons, were particularly helpful to her, always willing to help mow the grass or shovel snow.

When the neighbor man bought a brand new pickup truck, he had to park it in their driveway, since they used half of the garage for storage. The boys always had friends coming and going. Dave lamented that the boys and their friends were always opening car doors into the side of his new truck making little dents and nicks or scratching it with their stuff.

Mom kindly offered that he could park at the end of her driveway. Dave accepted, and started parking in mom's drive.

A couple weeks later, mom had already forgotten about Dave parking in her driveway. Backing her car out of the garage, she smashed into the front of his truck.

Father, please give us kind hearts. We want to always be willing to help others even when plans go awry.

Song Thoughts

"Just as I am and waiting not to rid my soul of one dark blot,
to thee whose blood can cleanse each spot."

> As iron sharpens iron, so a friend sharpens a friend.
> As workers who tend a fig tree are allowed to eat the
> fruit, so workers who protect their employer's interest
> will be rewarded. (Proverbs 27:17–18 NLT)

Walking regularly is always good exercise. My friend and I liked to walk together a couple evenings each week. We enjoyed the activity and getting outside, but even more we enjoyed the fellowship and the chance to talk with each other.

I watched her first-born grandson in my daycare. She hosted a baby shower for me prior to the birth of my daughter. Having a gift for gab, I corresponded with her son while he was serving overseas in Afghanistan.

Each Saturday morning my friend would come and pick me up so we would go to a Jazzercise class together. Dear me! I'm not sure whose idea it was. We always had quite a workout, not to mention a few good laughs. Afterwards, we would practically collapse next-door while having a doughnut or two. Ha ha. We hadn't had our talking time yet.

My friend lives in Florida now, but I see her son at church when we're visiting in Ohio. He bought one of my devotional books for her as a Christmas present. She was surprised and tickled. She says she loves it.

Thank you, heavenly Father, for our many friends in Christ and the blessings we share. Please continue to guide us as we share our love by helping each other, and being there in times of need as well as during relaxation.

Song Thoughts

"Your promise still stands. Great is your faithfulness.
I'm still in your hands. You've never failed me yet."

75—Working Hobbies

> He and all his family were devout and God-fearing; he
> gave generously to those in need and prayed to God
> regularly. (Acts 10:2 NIV)

Would you possibly be able to come help me put new brakes on my Jeep? I could probably do it, but I don't have all the tools I need, and since you have the tools? I need front and back.

My wife took our van to be checked before driving to Florida. We're going to her parents for spring break. They told her that we need new brakes.

I need new wheel bearings. I know you did them last year, but the guy at Honda said sometimes you just get bad parts. That's happened to them sometimes, and then they don't last as long as they should.

Do you think you could look at our refrigerator? The water dispenser doesn't work. At first, no one would look at it because they said it's digital. Finally, I got a repairman to come, and he said that I needed a whole new door.

Daddy, I just have a couple questions about our income tax. I figured you'd know.

Thank you, Father, for families. Thank you for the talents you give us so we are able to help each other in times of need.

Song Thoughts

"You're a good, good father. It's who you are, it's who you are.
It's who you are and I'm loved by you."

76—Somebody's Watching

In everything set them an example by doing what is good. In your teaching show integrity, seriousness and soundness of speech that cannot be condemned, so that those who oppose you may be ashamed because they have nothing bad to say about us. (Titus 2:7–8 NIV)

I was actively involved in our church. I sang in the church choir as well as another younger singing group called, Sounds of Joy. I worked part-time in the church's office, volunteered to help in the nursery, and usually helped with Vacation Bible School, too.

One day I asked our minister whether or not we had a regular gathering of any kind, just for single people. His reply was, "No we do not, but why don't you start one?"

Encouraged by his words and knowing the need, I set out to do just that. I was a single mom. I wanted a place to meet with others who could relate to my situation.

I had no clue as to even where to start. I'm not really sure how it happened, but one thing led to another, and we soon had an active singles group called 'Won by One.' God was leading the way.

That spring, my daughter's Girl Scout troop marched in the annual Memorial Day Parade. As I walked down the streets of the town with the troop leader and all the girls, I heard someone yell "Yay, Worthington Christian Church." My eyes tried to quickly search the crowd of people. I didn't see anyone that I knew or recognized, but they knew me.

Father, please help us to always be good examples to others in whatever we say or do and to everyone who sees us. Help us to remember that someone is always watching us.

Song Thoughts

"Jesus, name above all names, beautiful Savior, glorious Lord."

77–Joy and Laughter

> He will once again fill your mouth with laughter and
> your lips with shouts of joy. (Job 8:21 NLT)

Being an avid reader, I read all the Hardy Boys books and Nancy Drew Mysteries that I could get my hands on. I don't remember all the stories, but I'm pretty sure that the boys shouted E-O-KEE to call each other in at least one story, if not more.

Thinking it was a pretty cool way to keep in touch, my older sister, also a reader, and I decided it would be our way to find each other. We'd play in the woods between our house and the neighbors, and occasionally in the strip mines behind my grandma's house. We'd traipse here and there often doing our own thing. When and if we wanted to find each other, we'd holler out E-O-KEE.

One day I was feeling kind of down and lonely, so I called my sister. When she answered, I just called out E-O-KEE. We both started laughing as she asked, "Whatever made you think of that?"

I'm not sure why it was in my mind, but I do know that when we hung up our phones, my heart was much lighter. It made me happy just smiling and talking together with my sister.

Thank you, Father, for our siblings and the gift of laughter. I continue to be amazed at all the things you made as part of our lives when you created us.

Song Thoughts

"Worthy of every song we could ever sing,
worthy of all the praise we could ever bring."

78—Rest and Relax

Come to Me, all you who labor and are heavy laden, and I will give you rest. Take my yolk upon you and learn from Me, for I am gentle and lowly in heart, and you will find rest for your souls. (Matthew 11:28–29 NKJV)

My youngest sister, all three of my daughters, and I went to Wrightsville Beach in North Carolina for a little vacation. Our family friend encouraged us to come visit her. She offered us a free place to stay plus she was only minutes from the ocean.

It was a nine and a half hour trip, but with two drivers the time went fast. Our starts were sometimes slow and jerky, since my sister didn't know how to drive a stick shift with a clutch, but we made it.

One day we even ventured 45 minutes further south to spend a day at Myrtle Beach. We browsed the little tourist shops and found t-shirts to buy for the memories.

All good things must come to an end, and the next afternoon we headed home. My sister wanted to stop in Washington, D.C., so we took the scenic route. In a few hours it was night time and everyone was sleeping. I tried to find a hotel, but there weren't any vacancies, so I just kept driving. Maybe we can stop in D.C. next time.

Thank you, dear Father, for times of relaxation and pleasure. Please help us to appreciate and enjoy each moment of every day.

Song Thoughts

"I keep falling in love with Him, over and
over, and over and over again."

79–Abundant Blessings

> So whether you eat or drink or whatever you do, do
> it all for the glory of God. (1 Corinthians 10:31 NIV)

A new group of businesses was built a few miles away from our home. The Golden Corral opened a restaurant, too, so we decided to give it a try. The food was good, and we enjoyed our meals.

My youngest daughter loved going there to eat. She enjoyed trying new things and was delighted to have so many items from which to choose. She wasn't a picky eater, though she had her favorites. Occasionally, she chose some things she had eaten the last time.

When we stopped there one day for lunch, my daughter disappointedly told me they didn't have the chicken she always got. We walked to the buffet tables and she pointed to the sign above the meat she always ate. F-I-S-H.

We just figured she had discovered fish and loved it. I assured her that it was the same as always.

"But I like their chicken, not fish," she said with a frown on her face. What's that line? It tastes like chicken!

We praise you for our abundance of food. Thank you for all of our blessings, food, families, faith, and friends.

Song Thoughts

"So amid the conflict whether great or small,
do not be discouraged. God is over all."

80—Everyone Is Welcome

> Go ye therefore, and teach all nations, baptizing them in the name of the Father, and of the Son, and of the Holy Ghost. Teaching them to observe all things whatsoever I have commanded you: and lo, I am with you always, even unto the end of the world. (Matthew 28:19–20 KJV)

Even when my grandson was little, I was often surprised by his references to God. He knows that God loves us, and that He is always watching over us.

My grandson is caring and loving. It thrills my heart to know he has a heart for God. I liked to call him 'my little preacher boy.'

One day I asked him if he had ever considered becoming a pastor. He told me that he had actually thought about it.

"And what did you decide?" I asked.

"I wouldn't know what to say." he replied. "When people came to church, I would start by saying, welcome. Thank you for coming. Then I'd have to say have a wonderful week. See you next Sunday."

Tee hee. That's a start.

Heavenly Father, we do not know the plans you have for our lives, but help us to trust in you knowing that you will guide us.

Song Thoughts

"Here I am to worship. Here I am to say that you're my God."

81—Making Good Decisions

> But blessed is the one who trusts in the Lord, whose confidence is in him. (Jeremiah 17:7 NIV)

It was time for the annual Snowball Dance. Being a freshman in high school, I was finally old enough to attend. A fellow student that sat in the seat in front of me since second grade invited me to go as his date. We were excited about this big event and agreed to attend together.

The evening of the dance, my friend and his mom finally arrived. She sent him to the door to get me, saying that she would turn the car around and be ready to go.

Moments after my date came to the front door, his mom came running behind him. She was crying out, "I'm stuck in the garden! I'm stuck in the garden!"

Everyone ran outside and looked towards our garden. No car there. She had driven across the extended front yard and into a little creek.

Thankfully, my mom was willing and able to take us to the dance. And, luckily, a tow truck driver was able to rescue his mom's car.

Heavenly Father, please guide us and give us wisdom. Help us to make the right choices.

Song Thoughts

"On Christ the solid rock I stand, all other ground is sinking sand."

82–Hold Tight

> But you are to hold fast to the Lord your God, as you have unto now. The Lord has driven out before you great and powerful nations; to this day no one has been able to withstand you. (Joshua 23:8–9 NIV)

It seemed like they lived out in the boonies alone, but truth be told, there's just not that many people living in the small towns of Alaska.

Their yard reminded me a tiny bit of my home in Ohio, where I spent my childhood years. They had a rope hanging from a tree with a buoy attached to the end. In order to jump on the rope, my daughter had to stand on a tree stump. Then, she was high enough to hop up a little to grab hold, and plop on top of the buoy while swinging out over the marsh. According to her, she was having a blast.

Since her dad wanted to give it a try, she convinced him that he should also start by standing on the stump. That was probably unnecessary, since he was at least a foot taller than her, but he complied. Unable to copy her leap, he lost his grip, crashed into a bush which cushioned his fall, and then continued to roll down the hill towards the swamp. We couldn't stop laughing.

Father, we need your guidance every day. Please help us to hold tight to you and your word Lord, no matter what fears we face.

Song Thoughts

"Our God, a firm foundation, our rock,
the only solid ground, we trust forever in your name."

83–Enjoy Life

> You who are young, be happy while you are young, and
> let your heart give you joy in the days of your youth.
> Follow the ways of your heart and whatever your eyes
> see, but know that for all these things God will bring
> you into judgment. (Ecclesiastes 11:9 NIV)

My daughter was excited to turn nine years old. She had been anticipating her birthday for several weeks.

The afternoon of her special day began at the athletic club with a swimming party. It made me smile to hear the laughter and girly screams as I watched them play in the water.

Her dad spent his time in the pool with nine little girls hanging on him, practically all at the same time. Good thing he and his friend had been working out at the gym regularly. His muscles were put to good use that day.

Feeling exhausted, after only a few hours, we headed home to eat a small meal followed by lots of dessert. The Tweety Bird cake, lovingly made for my daughter by her talented aunt, along with some ice cream caused more laughing and screaming. The commotion and noise continued as my daughter opened her birthday presents, exclaiming over each gift.

The hustle and bustle finally seemed to be tapering off. It was time for the sleepover part. The girls happily put on their pajamas and slowly crawled into their sleeping bags. Whew! Goodnight.

Then we heard more laughter and screams. A few hours later, my husband asked, "Does this go on all night?"

Father, we are so blessed by the many joys in our lives. We know that every good and perfect gift comes from you.

Song Thoughts

"Strength will rise as we wait upon the Lord
our God, our hope, our strong deliverer."

Behold, children are a heritage from the Lord, the fruit of the womb is a reward. Like arrows in the hand of a warrior, so are the children of one's youth. Happy is the man who has his quiver full of them. (Psalm 127:3–5 NKJV)

My mom was an excellent seamstress. I might be mistaken in saying this, but I'm pretty sure that she always made the clothes we wore for holidays or special occasions.

I remember going to the fabric store in the fall to pick out material so mom could make our back to school outfits. We'd usually get new shoes for school, too, since our feet were always growing.

I fondly remember one Easter Sunday, probably due to the numerous pictures I've seen, that my mom made all five of us girls matching outfits. That year, she not only made my sisters and me beautiful dresses, we had look-a-like coats that mom sewed. In addition, mom and dad splurged for patent leather shoes and little white gloves, as well as Easter bonnets.

When dad grabbed his camera, we knew we were pretty as a picture. It was said that we looked like five little stair steps as our family walked into the church building that day!

Heavenly Father, thank you for the families in which you've placed us. Help us to trust you for the plans you have for our lives. Lord, we praise your name.

Song Thoughts

"I'm so glad I learned to trust Him, Precious Jesus, Savior, friend."

85—Someday We Will Understand

> For now we see only a reflection as in a mirror; then we
> shall see face to face. Now I know in part; then I shall
> know fully even as I am fully known. (1 Corinthians
> 13:12 NIV)

I went to visit my mom in the hospital. Moments after I said hello, lights began flashing and the alarms went off on her monitors. Doctors and nurses rushed into her room almost immediately. They asked me to leave, suggesting I go down the hall to the waiting room.

Worried and distraught, I walked out the door and burst into tears. Leaning against the wall, I allowed myself to slide down and sit on the floor. Walking any farther never entered my mind as I sat there broken-hearted, praying, and thinking that my mom was gone.

Finally feeling better, my mother asked them to let me come into her room. They told her that I had gone down the hall. She assured them I was right outside the door weeping. The hospital staff opened the door and looked down at me with amazed faces. They said I could come back into her room.

Then mom told me about her out of body experience, saying that she watched them work on her body from a corner of the ceiling. She also saw the former minister of our church who had died a few years earlier. He stretched out his hand wanting her to take hold. Mom said that she shook her head and told him that her daughters still needed her.

Your plans for our lives truly are a mystery, Lord. Thank you for the power of prayer and for always being with us every moment.

Song Thoughts

"And those who see must stand in awe for miracles abound.
I believe in miracles, for I believe in God."

86—Fellow Christians

> In the same way, let your light shine before others, that
> they may see your good deeds and glorify your Father
> in heaven. (Matthew 5:16 NIV)

We almost always sat in the same pew each Sunday, pretty much near the same people. And, ordinarily my little girl went to a Sunday school class. This week everyone was together for the same service and things were different.

Knowing she should be quiet, but getting tired of sitting still, my daughter began playing with the little ponytail of Ted, the gray haired man sitting in the pew in front of us. I quickly apologized to him but he said he did not mind at all and encouraged her to continue. Tee hee. (My daughter actually became a Cosmetologist.)

Recently, Ted passed away unexpectedly. Many people shared their sweet stories during the funeral about what a good Christian man Ted had been.

Concluding the service, after everyone else had finished, Ted's wife told one final story. She said that Ted went to the bank each week to get new bills for his tithe. Sometimes they didn't have sufficient new ones and the bank had to give him a few older wrinkled ones. When that happened Ted took them home and ironed them before putting them into his tithing envelope. Ted always wanted to give the best that was possible to the Lord.

Heavenly Father, please fill all of us with the desire to always give our best to you each and every day of our lives.

Song Thoughts

"Give of your best to the Master.
Give him first place in your heart.
Jesus has set the example."

87–Coming Together

> How good and pleasant it is when God's people live
> together in unity! ...For there the Lord bestows his
> blessing, even life forevermore. (Psalm 133:1,3 NIV)

The whole community worked together to have a very nice, brand
new swimming pool built in their park. They even had an over-sized
hot tub made outside the pool at the one corner.

The Lion's Club sponsored a day of festivities at the park in order to
announce and celebrate the grand opening of the swimming pool. All
the churches in the town agreed to meet together for one joint worship
service to be held that morning. It was so well attended they had to keep
adding more seats. What a great problem!

Since we were in Germany on the Sunday they were celebrating, we
went to church in the park with our family. The local band, in which
my brother-in-law plays, provided the accompaniment for the songs
during the worship service. They also played music during the luncheon
afterwards.

There was food, including desserts and beverages galore. Activities
went on throughout the day. They even had some giant water walking
inflatable Zorb balls for people to try. The kids loved them.

Heavenly Father, it is truly a day of celebration when those that
love you can put aside any differences and work together, ultimately
worshipping you, united in faith.

Song Thoughts

"We gather together to ask the Lord's blessing.
Beside to guide us, our God with us joining."

88—Friendly Neighbors

> Therefore encourage one another and build each other up, just as in fact you are doing. (1 Thessalonians 5:11 NIV)

I love being outside and riding my battery-powered scooter around the block. I enjoy meeting new people in our neighborhood and chatting with the ones that I already know.

When we first moved to this development, one family had a garage sale. I stopped by to browse and introduce myself.

Several years went by before we actually saw each other again and had the opportunity to talk. We refreshed each other's memories with our names. I thought that I remembered her husband's name was Frank.

She responded, "No, his name is Hank, but it is okay if you want to call him Frank." She continued, "That's what his grandma calls him, Frank, and his grandma even knows his real name!" Tee hee.

Then there are my new neighbors across the street. They told my husband and me that their names are Donny and Marie, but their last name is not Osmond. Hmm.

I met another young couple, too. By the second time I saw them, I had already forgotten his name. I remembered her name since it's the same as one of my daughters. I didn't want him to tell me his name, but I asked him to give me a hint, like what letter his name started with, in hopes that I could remember.

He laughingly said, "It starts with a J." Then I also had to laugh, because I remembered that his name was Jay.

Heavenly Father, thank you for all the people you bring into our lives. Please help us to be good friends and neighbors so that others can see you in our lives.

Song Thoughts

"I believe in God our Father, I believe in Christ the Son."

89—Family Fun

> She gets up while it is still night; she provides food
> for her family and portions for her female servants.
> (Proverbs 31:15 NIV)

We went to visit my mother-in-law in Germany. She was going to be celebrating her 80th birthday!

As always, Mama Anni was tickled to have us in her home. She insisted that Michael and I have her bedroom while she slept in the guest room each night. We could get up early or sleep late, but breakfast was always ready for us.

Each morning she rode her bike to the local bakery to buy fresh rolls. We had fresh strawberries everyday as well as bananas and kiwis. She made Michael's favorite meals from childhood. She spoiled us terribly the entire time we were with her.

Mama Anni even offered her favorite recliner as a seat to me. She was always willing to help us carry things, buy something, or explain directions. She wanted to show us, especially me, any places, palaces, or parks that I hadn't seen. We were treated like royalty.

On our last evening in Germany we enjoyed a big family gathering with dinner together at one of her favorite restaurants. Two of Mama Anni's friends joined us and happily took numerous family snapshots for all of us to enjoy. It's fun to look at the pictures and reminisce.

Thank you, Lord, for our families, our many blessings, and the love we share for each other.

Song Thoughts

"I'm so glad I'm a part of the family of God.
I've been washed in the fountain,
cleansed by His blood."

90—He Watches Over Us

For I am the Lord your God who takes hold of your
right hand and says to you, Do not fear; I will help you.
(Isaiah 41:13 NIV)

Our daughter in Ohio watched our cat, Honey Bear, while we went to
Germany. We had to fly from Columbus to Newark, New Jersey, to
catch our flight to Oslo, Norway and on to Frankfurt.

It was a very windy day when we boarded the plane, but the pilot
quickly flew above the turbulence. Even though I'm prone to motion
sickness, I did very well until we began our descent, and the flight got
very rough and bumpy.

My husband, always taking meticulous care of me, grabbed a couple
extra barf bags, just in case I might need them. Thankfully, we landed
soon. It felt great to stand on solid ground again. I was fine for the
remainder of our trip.

We had a wonderful visit in Germany. The morning we were to
leave, Michael woke up not feeling well. Prior to boarding the plane, we
decided to postpone our trip.

Then my husband changed his mind, and said that we should still
go. By the time we tried to rebook, our seats had been given to someone
else. We had to sit further back in the plane. Still not feeling well, my
husband had to use the bags he had taken for me.

We arrived in Sweden to find out that our flight had been delayed
for two hours. They gave us vouchers to get some food. After drinking
a bottle of Coca Cola, my husband felt better.

We missed our flight out of Chicago, but eventually we made it back
to Ohio and then safely home to New York.

Thank you, Father, for always being with us and watching over us.
We know you are beside every moment of every day. We praise you.

Song Thoughts

"Be not dismayed whate'er betide, God will take care of you."

91—Finding Solitude

> Then, because so many people were coming and going that they did not even have a chance to eat, he said to them, "Come with me by yourselves to a quiet place and get some rest." (Mark 6:31 NIV)

I love traveling to different countries. I never cease to be amazed at this beautiful world God has created for us to enjoy. When my husband and I visit his mother who lives in Germany, we try to get out and about to see new things.

On our most recent trip, after a couple rainy days in the Alps, we realized we could not see as far as usual, nor could we take any beautiful pictures. We decided to go home to Mama Anni's and spend more time with her.

Since there wasn't any rain in her town, the three of us went to a nearby park where we were able to enjoy the sunshine and walk around a beautiful lake. There were lots of trees and many varieties of lovely wildflowers. There were a few benches here and there along the water's edge inviting us to sit down and simply relax. It was very calm and peaceful.

Watching all the swans and numerous ducks was delightful. It was even more fun to toss them little pieces of bread. They loved it. I did, too.

Returning home to America, we went to church on Sunday. The sermon series was on Finding Solitude. What an appropriate reminder.

Father, it's so easy allowing ourselves to get caught up in the hustle and bustle of today's world. Thanks for the little reminders that help us remember to be still and draw closer to you.

Song Thoughts

"Indescribable. You are amazing God.
Awestruck we fall to our knees."

92—Do What Is Right

> You know the commandments: 'You shall not murder, you shall not commit adultery, you shall not steal, you shall not give false testimony, you shall not defraud, honor your father and mother.' (Mark 10:19 NIV)

I was so excited to finally go to school and be in first grade. We started each day by singing the <u>Good Morning to You</u> song. We're all in our places, with sunshine-y faces...

Our class then stood and faced the flag. We placed our right hands over our hearts and recited the <u>Pledge of Allegiance</u> together. Afterwards, we bowed our heads and prayed <u>The Lord's Prayer </u>in unison.

Occasionally, we had 'feets up' day. One of our fellow classmates often neglected to ask to go to the restroom, and a yellow stream went down the aisle between our seats.

After school we had just enough time to visit <u>The Little Store</u>. That was actually its name. We could zip in there to buy a piece of candy before hopping onto the bus to ride home.

One rainy day my mom allowed me to take her pretty umbrella to school. After school, I rushed into the store standing the wet umbrella in the corner by the front door. After purchasing my candy I went to hurry outside, but mom's umbrella was gone. I had to run through the rain to board my school bus.

Please forgive anyone who steals. Help us to forgive them, too. We pray that you will soften our hearts and help us to do what is right.

Song Thoughts

"A thousand times I failed, still your mercy remains,
and should I stumble again I'm caught in your grace everlasting."

93—Rejoice, Rejoice

> I know that nothing is better for them than to rejoice,
> and to do good in their lives, and also that every man
> should eat and drink and enjoy the good of his labor—
> it is the gift of God. (Ecclesiastes 3:12–13 NKJV)

My daughter, her husband, and their two young children came to visit us in New York. They had just spent a few days at Niagara Falls. Trying to get an early start in driving to our house, my daughter asked my granddaughter if she was awake.

"Well, my eyes are open." she responded.

Their first day here was very hot, so we let the kids run through the Crazy Flower sprinkler in the backyard. They were having a ball, getting wet and cooling down. They posed for pictures, turning cartwheels and acting silly.

After running around, laughing and screaming for almost an hour, my granddaughter ran over to me, asking, "Did I hear you say when we were done playing out here in the sprinkler that we were going to have some ice cream?"

"I did say that." I replied with a smile.

"Well, I'm actually done." She said.

Heavenly Father, I can only imagine all the things you have prepared to bring us joy in Heaven. Thank you so much for our numerous blessings. We love you Lord.

Song Thoughts

"There shall be showers of blessings.
Mercy drops round us are falling."

> Then Esau looked up and saw the women and children. "Who are these with you?" he asked. Jacob answered, "They are the children God has graciously given your servant." (Genesis 33:5 NIV)

It had been another long, hot and sweaty day. While my daughter's family was here we tried to do a lot of sightseeing. We almost shopped till we dropped, too.

Everyone was taking their baths or showers that evening around the same time, since we have three bathrooms. Once we were all in our pajamas, we were going to watch the movie 'Elf' that the kids had chosen.

Someone knocked on my bathroom door. I asked who it was, and inquired if they needed something. No one answered.

I learned afterwards that my grandson had been looking for me to ask about having popcorn during the movie. His mom told him that I was getting ready for bed, too.

My grandson asked if I was in the shower. Before his mom could answer, his sister quickly told him, "No, Nanny takes a bath. She might fall down in the shower and hurt herself."

Thank you, Father, for the smiles that little ones bring to our faces! Please show us how to make the most of every moment as we pass along our faith to them.

Song Thoughts

"I know not why his amazing grace to me he has made known.
But I know whom I have believed, and am persuaded that he is able."

95—Sharing With Others

> But do not forget to do good and to share, for with such
> sacrifices God is well pleased. (Hebrews 13:16 NIV)

I love watermelon and we hadn't eaten any yet this summer. So, when I saw the special sale price and a stock boy at the grocery store loading up a huge bin with watermelons, I asked him to please put one into my grocery cart. He happily complied with my request.

When I opened my refrigerator door, and saw that huge watermelon sitting there, my taste buds watered. My husband finally carved it. It made a big watery mess, but it was so delicious! We ended up with two large bowls of melon balls and two zip lock bags filled with individual slices. My husband agreed when I suggested we give some to our friends.

The next day I headed out to my neighbors on my battery-powered scooter with two bags of melon slices in my basket. Of course, they weren't home.

I enjoy being outside to catch a few rays, so I continued around the block. Two guys were refurbishing a house. I had seen them before, and they always waved. They waved this time, too, so I headed up the driveway. One guy was using an electric saw and wiping the sweat off of his forehead. I asked if he would like some watermelon, lifting up the bag I had.

Taking the offered slices, he said, "Thanks. There's nothing like some cold watermelon on a hot sunny day. You're the best. My name is Paul."

"Mary. Enjoy! Have a great day." I replied as I left.

It does my heart good to be a blessing to others, even in small ways. Showing kindness to Paul and his co-worker made my day. Thank you, Lord.

Song Thoughts

"It's your kindness, Lord that leads us to repentance.
Your favor, Lord, is our desire."

96–A Good Daddy

Start children off on the way they should go, and even when they are old they will not turn from it. (Proverbs 22:6 NIV)

My dad actively spent time with my sisters and me. I remember learning how to swim in an abandoned strip mine.

Traipsing through the woods on one of his hunting escapades, dad found a big pool of water. He cleared out the weeds and growth he found under the water, estimating it to be about nine feet deep.

Then, Dad built a nice size dock. He even made us a rustic diving board, so we could jump off of it.

We sat in old inner tubes, floating around in the water or we put it under our arms and learned to kick our feet. The day finally came when dad told us to forget the tube and climb onto his back. With a minimal amount of fear, we grabbed hold of his neck and went out into the deeper water.

When Dad said let go, we dog paddled like crazy and impressed ourselves. We knew Daddy was nearby, if we needed assistance. Our swimming talents improved over the years.

In the winter, when the water froze, dad taught us all how to ice skate. He built some log benches for us to use, not that we ever sat on them much. We were too busy ice skating. Dad even built a small campfire, in case we needed it to warm up. That rarely happened either. 'Wish I still had all that strength and energy!

Heavenly Father, we so often fail to recognize all the blessings you give us day after day. Thank you, Lord, for everything, especially the gift of Jesus and eternal life.

Song Thoughts

"Every blessing you pour out, I'll turn back to praise.
Blessed be the name of the Lord."

97–All That I Need

> Let the fields be jubilant, and everything in them; let
> all the trees of the forest sing for joy. (Psalm 96:12 NIV)

Michael and I were gone for three weeks. We had a lot of yard work that needed to be done when we returned from our trip. Actually there were lots of necessary things on our 'to do' list, like wash clothes, buy groceries, sort through the mail, etc.

We all know that it is fun to go places, but it's always nice to come home. We needed some rest and relaxation.

Sitting in the shade of the trees, near the flowerbeds, pulling weeds was very peaceful. Even though I was working, it felt refreshing. It was fun to help cut grass with the riding lawnmower, too.

The very next day, I happened to read an article that said, "Two hours a week in nature can boost your health and well-being." Researchers found that the results were consistent with ages, sexes, and areas. This even included people dealing with long-standing illnesses or diseases like MS.

I don't know about you, but I feel closer to God when I'm out in nature. I love the trees, flowers, lakes, oceans, blue skies and animals. A soft, gentle, rain is nice, too, especially when I want to take a nap or read a book.

Thank you so much, heavenly Father, for all the beautiful things that you created in this world for us to enjoy. We're in awe of you.

Song Thoughts

"What a beautiful name it is, nothing
compares to this, the name of Jesus."

98–Wear Love

> Give and it will be given to you. A good measure,
> pressed down, shaken together and running over, will
> be poured into your lap. For with the measure you use,
> it will be measured to you. (Luke 6:38 NIV)

My neighbors and I like to get together and chat. We're often sharing things that are going on in our lives as well as recipes. Times spent together are always fun. Occasionally, we treat each other to lunch or ice cream at the local shop nearby or in our homes to return a kindness that has been shown.

One friend loaned us their power sprayer to clean off our porch. My husband helped our neighbor hook up the water filter on their new refrigerator. I closed some windows and turned off a couple lights my neighbors forgot about before they left home. Another neighbor invited us to swim in their pool. I let a utility man into their house for my neighbors during their absence.

Just recently, I mentioned that my daughter, her husband, and their two young children were coming for a visit. The kids are eight and five years old.

My next door neighbor gave me two Barbie dolls from years ago for my little granddaughter. Cinderella and Rapunzel had never even been taken out of their boxes.

Another friend gave my grandson two Spider-Man action figures, a Pikachu (Pokémon) Creature, and a Marvel comic character.

My grandchildren will be thrilled. I'm anxious to see their excitement. I can hardly wait to see their smiling faces no matter! Tee hee.

Heavenly Father, we are so blessed. You give all of us so much everyday! Thank you for your goodness and generosity. No matter what else we wear, help us to always wear love.

Song Thoughts

> "Your name is great and your heart is kind,
> for all your goodness I will keep on singing,
> ten thousand reasons for my heart to find."

99—Relax and Trust in the Lord

> By the seventh day God had finished the work he had
> been doing; so on the seventh day he rested from all
> his work. Then God blessed the seventh day and made
> it holy, because on it he rested from all the work of
> creating he had done. (Genesis 2:2–3 NIV)

We were going to fly to Germany to help celebrate my mother-in-law's
80th birthday. There were lots of decisions to be made like what do
we pack? Should we take one big suitcase or two smaller ones? Will we
need warm clothes or things for a hot day? Do I take my scooter and my
walker? Should we hire the neighbor boy to mow our grass? Who should
we have watch our cat? So many things were swirling through my mind.

A few days later, we finally boarded our plane, only to sit there for
quite a while. As sometimes happens, we were awaiting clearance for
our plane to take off. Our plane slowly drove around the runway several
times. After about six or seven minutes a little boy on the plane called
out to his parents, "Are we flying yet?"

Everyone within hearing distance laughed. One lady even responded,
saying, "That's a good question."

Heavenly Father, we know that time is in your hands. Life seems to
pass in a flash while some things seem to take forever. Please help us to
relax and appreciate each moment, trusting in you.

Song Thoughts

"But until then my heart will go on singing.
With joy I'll carry on, until the day God calls me home."

100—Doing My Best to Show Love

> I love the Lord because he hears my voice and my prayer for mercy. Because he bends down to listen, I will pray as long as I have breath! (Psalm 116:1–2 NLT)

Several ladies in our church volunteered to have a beauty parlor day at the nursing home across the street. We agreed to wash and style the hair for any of the residents who wanted to participate.

All the ladies living there were thrilled to have our help and a day of pampering. I washed, dried, and curled the hair of several ladies. As time drew to an end, everyone started meandering down the hallways to their rooms.

Finishing the hairdo of my last little lady, I picked up the glasses lying nearby and helped her put them on her face. She gazed into the mirror admiring her fresh new look. Saying good-bye and telling me thank you, she went to join the others, smiling and patting her hair. Suddenly I heard her friend say, "Donna, you don't wear glasses."

"I don't?" she responded with a questioning look.

Heavenly Father, we thank you for the many opportunities we have to reach out and help others. Please fill us with the desire to want to show our love, especially to those less fortunate.

Song Thoughts

"Amazing love, how can it be that you my king would die for me."

101—Praise the Lord

> Even youths grow tired and weary, and young men
> stumble and fall; (Isaiah 40:30 NIV)

We did so much when my daughter's family came to visit. Our moments of relaxation were minimal. Lots of walking was involved such as running up and down the stairs in our home, playing in the sprinkler and doing some shopping at our favorite stores.

On their last full day here, we all got up early in order to take a trip to New York City so we could take in all the sights. One place on their list of things to see and do was the 9-11 Memorial. You could spend the entire day, maybe even a whole week, walking around inside that building to see everything as well as listening to all the audio information available. We were there a couple hours.

Of course, one has to ride the ferry out to see the Statue of Liberty up close so a bunch of pictures can be taken. And, you can't forget to buy a souvenir from the gift shop.

The morning they were loading up their suitcases and things to leave for Ohio, my granddaughter gave me a big hug and said, "I'm really tired. When I get in Daddy's car to drive home, I'm going to fall asleep for ten minutes. Mommy's going to have to wake me up when we get home."

I didn't have the heart to tell her it was more like a ten hour trip driving to Ohio from eastern New York.

Time can be fleeting, Father. Please help us to use every day according to your plan for our lives. We want to be a light to the world.

Song Thoughts

"But now I am happy – securely I rest; No longer I roam
my soul faces home, I walk and I talk with the King."

102–Special Friends

> Therefore, as God's chosen people, holy and dearly loved, clothe yourselves with compassion, kindness, humility, gentleness and patience. (Colossians 3:12 NIV)

When I moved to Worthington, I started looking for someone from whom I could buy Mary Kay cosmetics. Not only did I find that person, I found a wonderful Christian friend. She persuaded me to sell MK, too.

We ended up being part of the same church. We shared our faith, and our lives, as we began walking and talking together. Eventually, I moved out of state though I still see my friend at church sometimes when we're visiting our family.

We were attending a special patriotic program that evening. I remember being in the church choir years ago when we sang the songs of each military branch. The men who served our country were asked to stand when we sang their song.

Even though they were no longer having the choir sing, I was excited to attend the annual patriotic program. In honor of the people who had served our country, they were going to show pictures of everyone in their service uniforms on a big screen up front.

Sitting in the pew behind me, my friend happily introduced me to her new husband. When his picture flashed across the screen, my friend leaned over to whisper, saying "Look how handsome he was!"

Smiling, I responded, "I think he's still good looking!"

"Thanks," he replied.

"That's what I meant to say," she said laughing.

Thank you, Father, for our wonderful Christian friends and for those who serve our country. They bring joy as well as laughter to our lives. Please help our faith in you continue to grow.

Song Thoughts

"Blest be the tie that binds our hearts in Christian love.
The fellowship is like that above."

103–Joyful Hearts

> Do your best to present yourself to God as one approved,
> a worker who does not need to be ashamed and who
> correctly handles the word of truth. (2 Timothy 2:15 NIV)

There were a lot of young families in our church. We had a very active congregation. Trying to make as many opportunities as possible for people to get involved in activities and spend time together, we started having a night called open gym at the middle school that was about a mile down the road from the church building.

I enjoyed going to gym night each week to join everyone in a game of volleyball. While the nets were being put up, some folks liked to shoot baskets. Several people, including our pastor, picked up a basketball. I watched as he tried about four or five times to make a basket. I laughed as his shot didn't even reach the rim, let alone the back board.

Hearing me giggle, he quickly threw the ball to me, saying, "Let's see you make one."

I shot the ball into the air towards the hoop. Swoosh! It dropped straight through the net, without touching the rim. Ha, ha.

It was purely luck on my part, though I'd had a lot of practice thanks to my dad. I had to smile as the pastor stood there in awe with his jaw hanging down.

Another great night playing volleyball happened when I blocked a spike hit by a guy who had a scholarship to play volleyball at Ohio State. Wow! I amazed myself. His compliment made me smile. I'm not sure it was worth the bruise that appeared on my wrist later, though. Ouch!

Father, you give us so many natural abilities and talents to bring joy to our lives, including the gift of laughter. We always want to live lives that please you. Thank you.

Song Thoughts

"Wonderful, wonderful, wonderful, wonderful,
isn't Jesus my Lord wonderful?"

104—Sisters, Sisters

> This is how we know who the children of God are and
> who the children of the devil are: Anyone who does not
> do what is right is not God's child, nor is anyone who
> does not love their brother and sister. (1 John 3:10 NIV)

I flew to Ohio for a family reunion. Not all extended family members could attend, but every one of my sisters came. We hadn't all been together for five years although we had talked individually via texts and telephones. I took a lot of pictures.

We sang our favorite songs, at least the ones that we could think of, loving the beautiful harmony. We laughed and shared our present lives as well as many fond memories. We ate tons of yummy food. Our time together passed way too quickly and we had to say our good-byes. I'm hoping we'll see each other again soon.

When I was in Boston at a Street Fair, I happened to see a female artist painting cute little 3 ½" X 4 ½" pictures of sisters or friends and giving each one a title. I loved the small picture showing five girls with big smiles on their faces. It read, "Side by side, or miles apart, sisters like us stay close to the heart."

I happily purchased one for each of my sisters and myself. Per my request, the artist painted each girl in the picture with the correct hair color and wrote our names underneath each picture. We all love the sweet memento.

So many blessings, our Father, and yet you continue to give us more each day. Thank you so much for your love as well as the love of friends and families. We look forward to reuniting in heaven with our loved ones.

Song Thoughts

"You didn't want heaven without us,
so Jesus you brought heaven down.
What could separate us now?"

105–Love and Kindness

> So God made the wild animals, the tame animals, and all the small crawling animals to produce more of their own kind. God saw that this was good. (Genesis 1:25 NIV)

When my son was about eight years old, he and his younger cousin saw several tiny baby frogs jumping around on the sidewalk. Thinking they were big bugs, his cousin quickly stomped on one. Sad and broken hearted, my son yelled at his cousin saying, "Didn't your mom ever teach you to be kind to animals?"

Years later, my brother-in-law set out a trap and caught a chipmunk. My sister planned to drive a few miles down the road to set it free into the wildlife preservation area.

Their grandson was visiting with them. My sister put the box into the trunk of her car and had her grandson get into his car seat. She hurriedly ran inside to grab her purse and car keys.

When she came back out, the empty trap box was sitting in the driveway. Her grandson was standing beside it with tears running down his cheeks, crying, "He had to be free."

Heavenly Father, we thank you for our children and grandchildren. Our hearts are touched by the love they demonstrate to us, and the concern they show for others, including animals.

Song Thoughts

"This is my Father's world. All nature sings
and round me rings the music.
In the rustling grass I hear him pass. He speaks to me everywhere."

106–Understanding

Your word is a lamp to my feet and a light to my path.
(Psalm 119:105 NKJV)

A friend I knew from high school had his pilot's license. He took me up in a two-seater airplane one day. It was fun and I had no fear until I realized we had to get back down somehow. I hoped and prayed he knew what he was doing!

Prior to my first flight in a big, commercial plane, I was a nervous wreck. Like my initial flight, we made it up and back down, landing safely. Finally, I was no longer afraid to fly after hearing that flying in a plane was safer than driving in a car!

On a recent flight coming home to New York from Ohio, I was looking out the window. Houses looked smaller and smaller until they were barely the size of a dot and I could not even see any people. That's when Psalm 103:13-14 (NIV) popped into my mind. "As a father has compassion on his children, so the Lord has compassion on those who fear him; for he knows how we are formed, he remembers that we are dust."

'Talk about a perfect image!

I love it, Lord, when your word and scriptures are made perfectly clear to me and I understand what you are saying. Your love for us is amazing.

Song Thoughts

"How firm a foundation, ye saints of the Lord, is laid for your faith in His excellent word. What more can He say, than to you He hath said."

107—Days in Our Lives

> You were taught, with regard to your former way of life …
> to put on your new self, created to be like God in true
> righteousness and holiness. (Ephesians 4:22,24 NIV)

Years ago my sister and I were in the Sears store. Our daughters started running in and out of the racks of clothes, chasing each other and hiding. My oldest daughter gashed her forehead open near the hairline. We grabbed the girls, jumped into my sister's car and zoomed down the freeway. Thankfully, the hospital was not very far away and my daughter was quickly attended to by the emergency room doctors.

The manager of the store had asked us to come back and fill out some paperwork for him. It's a good thing we agreed to return, because I had left my purse sitting on the checkout counter by the cash register. No one touched it and all of my things, including my wallet, were still inside my purse.

Another day, my kids all went to the swimming pool. I was home alone. I contacted one of my good friends. She ended up driving over for a visit and we went to have ice cream cones. When I thanked her for coming to see me she responded, "We need to do this while we have the opportunity. No one knows what might happen tomorrow."

Almighty God, our lives and the time we spend here on earth are in your hands. You number our days just as you pour out our blessings. We give thanks and praise your name.

Song Thoughts

"When the trumpet of the Lord shall sound
and time shall be no more.
When the roll is called up yonder, I'll be there."

About the Author

Mary was one of five girls and grew up in the small town of East Canton, Ohio. She is the proud mother of one son and three daughters, all happily married. Mary has fourteen fantastic grandchildren.

Mary and her husband, Michael, met in Ohio, and currently live in upstate New York. They're hoping to return to Ohio when Michael retires. Mary says 'once a Buckeye, always a Buckeye' plus her heart will always be in Ohio where most of her family resides.

Mary loves to read, write, and sing. She also enjoys watching the Ohio State Football team play every year. Go Bucks!

Printed in the United States
By Bookmasters